IFP

INTERNATIONAL FOCUS PRESS

IF ONLY I HAD
KNOWN

A True Story

IF ONLY I HAD
KNOWN
—— *A True Story* ——

WILLIAM H. DODSON, PH.D.

IFP
INTERNATIONAL FOCUS PRESS
RICHARDSON, TEXAS

Published by
Interational Focus Press
P.O. Box 831587, Richardson, Texas 75083-1587
www.ifpinc.com

ISBN 978-0-9893358-0-5

Library of Congress Control Number: 2009932274

For quantity purchases, please contact
International Focus Press.

With the advent of the Internet and late-breaking stories, source information
was not available for all images, especially from some foreign websites.
Appropriate attrubution will be provided on the IFP Live Addendum
page for this book and in subsequent printings/editions as it is obtained.

1. School Violence 2. Education 3. Crime 4. Criminology
5. Violence in Society 6. Crime Prevention 7. Current Events

Printed in the United States of America

Second Printing May 2013

CONTENTS

IMPORTANT UPDATE FOR SECOND PRINTING

Regrettably, this update is necessary because of two horrific massacres last year. The first occurred on July 19, 2012, in suburban Aurora, Colorado, during a midnight showing of a new Batman movie, *The Dark Knight Rises*, killing 12 and wounding 58. The killer was only 24 years old. The second massacre took place on December 14 at Sandy Hook Elementary School in Newtown, Connecticut. The 20-year-old killer took the lives of 20 children, 6 staff, and wounded 2 others before killing himself (he murdered his mother earlier in the day). Both killers had the Random Actor profile, explained in Chapter 8. This profile was developed by Dan Korem, introduced in Chapter 1.

If 100 teachers, selected at random from the over 15,000 teachers who have been trained to identify the Random Actor traits, were shown video footage of these killers when they were teens, they would have been identified and Korem's three-point intervention (Chapter 9) that has saved countless lives would have been immediately provided.

It was anticipated that a second edition of this book would be released next year, but because of these events and the severely escalating number of threats and attacks, important data collected by Korem is included in this update and Chapter 8 in the hope of saving lives.

6% of K–12 and higher education students have the Random Actor profile. Most will not kill or harm, but globally virtually every student mass school killer has this profile. Before the 1999 Columbine Massacre, the highest estimate Korem would release was 1–2%, although thousands of educators, school psychologists, and counselors said it was higher. He revised the estimate because a major 2009 federal study (the United States Preventative Task Force) found that 6% of all students are clinically depressed. Today, when Random Actor violence prevention strategies are applied in schools, the 6% number has proven accurate. Since the late 1990s, Korem warned that unless intervention was applied as detailed in this book, we would see horrific Random Actor slayings by young people as they enter the adult population, like the attacks in Newtown, Aurora, and others at Virginia Tech University (2007), the University of Northern Illinois (2008), and the first suicide bombing at the University of Oklahoma (2005).

Over 250 times a day during the school year students are found with guns, bombs, and plots to take out their schools. Around the time of the Columbine Massacre, there were about 50 of these threats a day (which doesn't include prank threats). As the number of students with the Random Actor profile continued to increase, so did the number of threats. By the time of the Batman Movie Massacre, it was about 100 times a day. Right after that attack, Korem called the executive director of the Texas Association of School Administrators, Dr. Johnny Veselka, who he regularly worked with since 1997 to help school districts successfully prevent attacks. He warned that the 2012–2013 school year would probably be the worst school year on record for threats and attacks. In the fall, threats escalated to about 150 a day. After the Newtown Massacre, they increased to over 250 a day, unprecedented in American history, and they persisted through the spring of 2013 as did Random Actor slayings in the general population. On January 10, right after schools reconvened, the first school attack of 2013 hit Taft, California, a small town, followed by many others.

Misconception #1: Most Random Actor killers are mentally ill. While some are, Korem's twenty years of experience is that most students aren't. While all are extremely fearful (as explained in Chapter 8), they don't necessarily have a DSM IV diagnosable condition. It's critical to recognize this because many mental health practitioners assume that if there isn't a diagnosable condition, there isn't the risk of committing a massacre. One of the Columbine killers, for example, was tested before the attack and no mental health condition was found, although he clearly had the Random Actor profile. Only 4% of all violent acts can be attributed to mental illness, according to a major study in the "American Journal of Psychiatry," Vol. 163, No. 8.

Misconception #2: Bomb proofing windows and banning guns will prevent massacres. Globally, almost all Random Actor school attacks have occurred in statistically safe and affluent communities—suburbs and small towns—and the schools usually had state-of-the-art security. The problem is that you can build explosives with materials that can be found *in* any school. What most don't realize is the Columbine killers intended to kill over 400 with two bombs placed *in* the cafeteria that never detonated. The day of the Newtown Massacre, China experienced another of its dozens of elementary school attacks by a Random Actor assailant with a knife, butchering over 25 children. So is China's solution to ban tableware? Of course not.

Regarding guns, if someone is intent on killing, there is no shortage of options: explosives, napalm, gas, etc. Many attacks have been thwarted where youth tried to use these materials. Regardless of one's stance on the Second Amendment, it's foolhardy to believe that merely limiting guns will reduce Random Actor attacks. (This week's April 15, 2013, attack during the Boston Marathon using bombs made from pressure cookers—found in most homes—is a sober reminder.) The only long-term proven method of preventing attacks is reaching students *before* they hatch a plot with the three-point intervention explained in Chapter 9.

Cautious Innovator profile added to the *Korem Profiling System*. This is an important addition (that supplements Chapter 8) and details about it can be found in Korem's book, ***The Art of Profiling—Reading People Right the First Time, 2nd ed.*** While there is nothing inherently destructive about the profile, it's the world's fastest growing one and understanding it retards false positives when identifying people with the Random Actor profile.

Specific terms have changed in the *Korem Profiling System* because language has changed. Unpredictable and Predictable (Chapter 8) are now Unconventional and Conventional. The terms are capitalized because they have a specific meaning as referenced in Chapters 8–10.

PREFACE

F or updates to *If Only I Had Known*, please refer to the "Live Addendum" page on the International Focus Press website (www.ifpinc.com). Also, this project is unusual in that the publisher, Dan Korem is also a contributor to Chapters 8, 9, and 10, which is adapted from his book *Rage of the Random Actor—Disarming Catastrophic Acts and Restoring Lives* (2005) and *The Art of Profiling—Reading People Right the First Time, 2nd ed.* (2012).

CHAPTER 1

Tragedy On My Watch

O n October 1, 1997, when I was superintendent of Pearl Public Schools in Jackson, Mississippi, Luke Woodham, a sixteen-year-old sophomore, stabbed and bludgeoned his mother to death, then took a rifle to Pearl High School and shot nine students. Two died; seven were wounded.

The act seemed to come out of the blue, with Luke Woodham randomly shooting anyone who moved. He did it in a usually safe and serene community.

And he did it on my watch.

That shocking day and its awful events are never far from my mind. It started an unsettling national wave of violence in otherwise placid neighborhoods and schools—in statistically safe suburbs and small towns. And it provoked a personal ten-year hunt to answer the question: What could we have done to prevent the attack? What did we miss?

Two months after the Pearl assault—December 1, 1997—a student attack in West Paducah, Kentucky, killed three students and injured five. On March 24, 1998, in a Jonesboro, Arkansas, attack, three students and one teacher were killed; ten were injured. On May 21, 1998, a high school shooter in Springfield, Oregon, killed two students as well as both his parents. Then on April 20, 1999, a massacre at Columbine High School in Littleton, Colorado, claimed the lives of fifteen—and the teenage gunmen committed suicide as law enforcement tried to secure the school.

Similar attacks have spread to Canada and European countries such as Germany, Finland, and Greece. To date, the largest high school attack took place in tranquil Erfurt, Germany, in 2002—where 16 students were slain. The greatest loss of life on a college campus took place at Virginia Tech in 2007, where 32 were slain.

Nationally, the Pearl attack caught the media's attention because it was the first in many years. There had been earlier school attacks in Bath, Maine (a bombing in 1927 by an adult), at the University of Texas (adult student sniper in the campus bell tower in 1966), and Moose Lake, Washington (teenager shooting attack, 1996). Those isolated incidents, though, didn't start a trend. The attack at Pearl High school changed that. It involved gang and satanic overtones led by a mastermind college student who preyed on the insecurities of younger high school students. It had the intrigue of devil worship, animal torture, home-grown gang crime, and the trial of six students charged as conspirators after the murder of Luke Woodham's mother and the school attack.

The Pearl incident and other school violence sparked national conferences and studies as well as a debate about guns on campus—because our assistant principal, an officer in a local National Guard unit, retrieved his pistol from his parked car and used it to apprehend Luke Woodham as he fled the school.

One of those studies, conducted by the FBI in 1999, concluded that we can't identify students who are likely to commit such violent attacks. The Secret Service and the Department of Education came to the same conclusion in a 2002 report. Millions of dollars were spent on those studies, and if they were right, I wouldn't have written this book.

The fact is that there *are* predictors:

First, we *can* identify most of these students—even before they ever think about committing a violent act—and without stereotyping or stigmatizing them.

Second, there *is* an intervention that guides most of these students out of harm's way.

Third, there are specific reasons that these incidents typically happen in the safest locales—suburbs and small towns—and almost never in the inner-city. Conversely, students in the nation's thousands of alternative discipline schools for *at-risk* students never hatch massacre plots. Think of it: a population of *only at-risk* schools that logically would be *most* likely to have an attack . . . yet, they rarely if ever suffer the attacks that "stable" schools experience. Paradoxical as it seems, it's a fact.

The purpose of this book is twofold. One, what happened to us at Pearl can happen in your community, even if it's considered safe, statistically—*especially* if it's considered safe, statistically. Two, there *is* something we can do.

While this isn't a "true crime" book, included here are vivid descriptions of the attack as provided by Pearl's assistant principal, Joel Myrick—who not only witnessed the attack but also armed himself and apprehended Luke Woodham, thus perhaps preventing further loss of life. His moment-by-moment account will put you at the scene and help you understand what we experienced. Also, a juror at one of Luke Woodham's trials, an educator with a doctorate and an emphasis in criminal justice, records her experience. Finally, I'll share my prison visits with Luke Woodham—and his responses when I asked him if there was anything we could have done to prevent the attack.

Those story threads are interesting, enlightening, and help flesh out this book's narrative. But the important story, as suggested above, is that there is a body of research aimed at recognizing and preventing these rampages. This research was conducted over twenty-plus years by investigative journalist Dan Korem, and his findings led him to predict in the early '90s the wave of school attacks that would follow. He specifically stated that the attacks would be committed by students with the Random Actor behavioral profile, a profile he developed as a component of the *Korem Profiling System* which was published in his book, *The Art of Profiling—Reading People Right the First Time.* We'll look at Korem's work[1] in greater detail later. For now, a broad outline of how he stumbled onto his two-decade course of research will suffice.

Imagine that you just solved the riddle of why there are mass shootings in the Post Office but not FedEx—even though both are in the delivery business. And you discovered not only what FedEx was doing differently from the USPS but also how to replicate those differences in any organization.

At the same time, you happened to be doing research for a book on suburban gangs . . . and you see a significant number of kids with the same profile as the postal shooter—traits you've now identified as the Random Actor profile.

What would you do?

You'd get the word out to schools—including how to apply FedEx's techniques to guide those at-risk students out of harm's way so they never commit an attack.

That's what Korem did.

He took his information to education and law enforcement professionals before the school attacks, warning them of the trend before it developed.

After the flurry of attacks that began with Pearl, many schools across the country deployed Korem's strategies. The results were stunning: attacks were averted, threats were reduced, building evacuations decreased, discipline/behavioral referrals of students with Random Actor traits diminished, and their classroom performance improved. (We'll discuss these strategies and results later.)

Since 1997, more than 15,000 educators and 5,000 law enforcement and military professionals have applied Korem's research with similar success. And, after 9/11, when thousands of students made terrorist threats against North American schools and thousands of schools temporarily closed, one region in the United States did not receive such threats. It was the only region that deployed Korem's violence prevention strategies in its schools.

It's now 2009 and the tenth anniversary of the Columbine massacre. Immediately before Columbine, schools received 25 to 50 authentic student attack threats with bombs or guns a day. Today, that number is 75 to 100 per day (see Chapter 8).

Also, 2009 saw the release of the nightmarish, true-crime book *Columbine*, which dispelled myths about the attack. Like other books on student-led attacks, though, it never answered the critical *why* questions. As far away as Ireland, Mary McCloskey in the *Irish Times* wrote a book review of *Columbine* entitled, "Study of Columbine killings that fails to address key question: Why?"

Because answers to the "why" questions aren't common knowledge among educators, media continue to propagate the myths. On April 20, 2009, for example, a *Dallas Morning News* columnist wrote in an article titled, "Lesson from Columbine is disturbingly simple":

The lesson should be that some people—mercifully, a very few —have such dark and mutated souls that they are capable of doing terrible and deliberate damage. Trying to stop them before the fact provokes the same civil rights debate that complicates efforts to prevent terrorism. If we tried to lock up every angry teenager with a creepy violence obsession, we wouldn't have a place to put them all. That's not the popular, ideologically elastic answer most people want. I'm afraid, though, it might be the only one there is.

In other words, most of these students are dark monsters—and we can't try to help them without violating their civil rights. That's a myth. Random Actor violence prevention strategies were used in Pearl after the Woodham attack, and we had neither lawsuit nor complaint. Neither have hundreds of schools or private and public sector organizations.

The reality is that students aren't stigmatized when certain strategies are appropriately applied. I've been an educator for over forty years and have learned that, just as with any other troubled student, you can reach out to students with the Random Actor profile without violating civil rights and unwarranted stereotyping.

I have no doubt that had we at Pearl identified students with Random Actor traits and applied Korem's intervention techniques, we would not have had an attack. I am also certain of something else: We must focus on *prevention* rather than on *reaction*. And in this book, I hope to share with you the recognition and prevention techniques that will keep you from walking in my shoes, lamenting *if only I had known . . . .*

CHAPTER 2

PEARL AND COLUMBINE
WORLDS APART — SAME RESULT

You never would have picked Pearl or Columbine High School as likely locales for campus rampages. It just doesn't make sense. Both schools are located in statistically safe suburban communities whose crime indexes are below state and national averages. Pearl is a suburban small town of over 20,000 just outside Jackson. Columbine High School is located in an unincorporated area of Jefferson County right next to Littleton, a Denver, Colorado, suburb of about 40,000. The cultures at Pearl and Columbine are different but the consistent theme is quality of life. Pearl is an affluent upscale community compared to the rest of Mississippi, but still small town at heart. The pace of life is a bit slower than in Littleton, the seventeenth most populated city in Colorado, which has more big-city sophistication.

Before you read about the attack at our high school, I want to compare my community with Littleton. If you also live in a suburb or small town, ask yourself, does this sound a little bit like my neighborhood?

Most Mississippi towns are small and unattractive compared to the larger American cities. Yet, there is a uniqueness about them that grows on a person after living here for a time.

In Mississippi the communities are small enough that most citizens know each other. There is a caring attitude among its residents. When someone dies the funeral homes are packed with those who want to express their sympathies.

The churches are packed each Sunday with worshippers wanting to be a part of their faith. They are alive with fellowship and togetherness. The most common socials are church and family reunions.

The name of our community, Pearl, comes from the Pearl River that separates the town from Mississippi's capitol city of Jackson. Currently, there are 22,000 residents and it is the largest city in Rankin County. It is immediately east of Jackson in the middle of the state and forty-five miles east of the Mississippi River.

Both Pearl and Rankin County have had colorful histories. During prohibition days a trip across the river bridge to Rankin County could secure any kind of alcoholic spirits that you wished to buy. The area was fondly called the "Gold Coast" for its spirits supply business to the Capitol City.

Liquor was hidden in the river in underwater containers to escape the state agents who canvassed the state to prevent the sale of illegal alcohol beverages, and Jackson citizens weren't shy about crossing the river bridge for their supply.

In the late 1960s, working folks in Jackson moved to the outlying areas to escape high taxes and big city government. The unincorporated town of Pearl petitioned the state for incorporated status. The city of Jackson fought the petition in court as it wanted to annex the area, but the Pearl petitioners were successful. The area became an incorporated city in June 1973—the largest unincorporated area in the state to petition for city status at that time.

The original size of the first incorporation was 11 square miles but after a number of annexations it soon grew to be 22 square miles.

The racial makeup of the city is 82 percent white, 16 percent African American and 2 percent other to include, Native Americans, Asians, and Hispanics. The median income for a family is $42,013 and the population below the poverty line per family is 9.2 percent. Our respect for diversity, distinct from our past, was evident as reflected by Chelsey Kelly, who was African-American and our homecoming queen.

Like Littleton, Pearl has been a boom town, steadily growing prior to and after our attacks. In 2005, we opened the 7,500 seat Trustman Park home of the Mississippi Braves, an AA minor league baseball team.

Once citizens grow up in Pearl, it is hard for them to leave. A high percentage of adults have lived in Pearl since childhood or birth. As superintendent of schools I have known families to decline job promotions out of state to stay in the city and allow their children to attend its schools.

A special quality in Pearl is the devotion of most families to their children. Many communities have adult activities such as civic clubs and country clubs as their focus. Pearl, however, centers its involvement on children and grandchildren. Youth programs are a priority. You can see that by the mini-vans driving family members and friends to band contests, choral music contests and athletic events. The parent support is the most important factor in the success of these children.

Because many of our students do not come from families that have excelled academically, the parents value a good education. The parents help by selling and producing items for fund raising events to pay for the numerous student activities in the schools.

Since its establishment in 1976, the Pearl school system has been one of Pearl's greatest assets. The school system has excelled in the arts, athletics, and academics since its inception, and our citizens have generously supported education bond issues, state-of-the-art buildings, classrooms, fields, and equipment.

We have three elementary schools, one junior high and one high school for our 4,000 students. Northside Elementary and Pearl High School received Blue Ribbon status as designated by the U.S. Department of Education. Pearl High had about 1,040 students in 1997. In 2005 the school system received the Governor's Award for Excellence in the Arts. Pearl High School is currently rated a 5, which is the highest educational level a school can reach based on the Mississippi Curriculum Tests. The school, a red brick postmodernist structure, is nicely landscaped, with ample physical activity areas including a football stadium, track and band facilities plus tennis courts. Built in 1987, it was constructed to house a capacity of 1,500 students. There are no residential or commercial structures within a mile of the site, and it is on a dead end street.

I moved to Pearl in 1982 from Greenville, a town in the Mississippi Delta. I was hired by the local school board to replace the first superintendent of schools, Henry Shephard. One of my daughters had already graduated from high school, and our other daughter, Susan, was an eighth grader. She joined the high school band as a high school freshman. The band was a great character builder for her and gave her confidence to become a good student.

What started out as only a place to advance in a new job turned into years of enjoyment among many friends and associates. My wife and I have settled into the community after both of our retirements.

Like the students at Columbine, Pearl students are fiercely competitive when opposition confronts them. The Pirates form one of Mississippi's best-known school rivalries with the Rankin County Brandon High Bulldogs. In past years the football teams have played in Jackson's Memorial Stadium because neither school's stadium can hold the overflow crowds that attend each year.

If you like a slower paced small-town suburban feel, you would feel right at home with your kids attending Pearl High.

If you'd like a bit more excitement with the background of the Rockies, you'd probably send your kids to Columbine.

The city of Littleton covers a 13.9 square mile area of land with a racial population of 92 percent white, 1.2 percent African American and other races to include small percentages of Native Americans, Asians, Hispanics, and Pacific Islanders. The median household income is $50,583 with 6 percent of the population below the poverty level.

Littleton also has a colorful history tracing its beginning to the "Pikes Peak" gold rush of 1869. Along with the gold-seekers came merchants and farmers to provide the necessities of life. One provider was Richard Little of New Hampshire, an engineer, who helped lay out ditches to drain water from the farms and businesses. The Littles became a prominent family in the area leading a settlement development that involved schools, churches and stores. In 1890 the village was incorporated as the Town of Littleton.

Columbine High School is located one mile west of the Littleton city limits and half a mile south of the Denver city line. The ZIP code of the school is associated with the city of Littleton. The school name Columbine comes from the state flower by that name. In 2009, the high school has an enrollment of 1,693 for grades nine through twelve. In 1999, the date of the shooting, the enrollment was 1,965.

The school went through a major remodeling four years before the shooting, adding a new library and cafeteria. After the massacre, the library where some of the shootings took place was demolished and the site was established as a memorial.

The school's most recent success has come from its excellent cheerleading squads and football teams, something that caught my eye as a former football coach. In 2006 the Rebels, as they are called, won the 5A State Football Championship played at Mile High Stadium, home of the NFL Denver Broncos. Like Pearl, Littleton was rarely in the news except in 1990, as Dan Korem explains in his book, *Rage of the Random Actor*:

> In reaction to an increase in gang violence, suicides, and teens killed while driving, Columbine was one of approximately 10 percent of U.S. high schools that opted to teach "death education." Elementary through high school students were taken to morgues, mortuaries, and funeral parlors to see, touch, and even smell cadavers to drive home the reality of death and hopefully that life was important. In some cases kids wrote out their own epitaph for their tombstone. On the surface the idea seemed like a good one to many educators, until cases emerged where it got out of control.
>
> An English literature teacher . . . integrated her personal beliefs on reincarnation and that "when you die you get all the knowledge that God has," one of her students, Tara Becker, recalled. From a two-parent home, as a Columbine junior in 1984, Tara had thoughts of suicide and battled depression. She never actually contemplated carrying out her suicidal impulse until her teacher presented the idea that death "was exciting . . . Something to look forward to . . . It was an escape. . . . The things we learned in the class taught us how to be brave enough to face death." Tara, now emboldened, planned her suicide, but her parents noticed something was wrong and took her to a hospital before she acted on her impulse. When *ABC's 20/20* covered the story, Littleton school officials refused to comment and said that what the teacher did had nothing to do with Tara's problems. This case and others . . . are what caused me to monitor the Denver suburbs and a handful of other U.S. locales that I believed were indicators of future at-risk juvenile trends to come.[1]

Littleton was at the front end of a suburban, small-town gang trend that Korem identified and wrote about in his 1994 book,

Suburban Gangs—The Affluent Rebels. It was only a short time later that Pearl joined the trend like most North American suburbs and small towns.

What most people still don't realize is that the Pearl attack was actually the end product of the formation of one of these home-grown suburban gangs Korem predicted in the mid-1980s would appear. The Pearl teen gang members were recruited by one of our local community college students. Luke Woodham was just one member of the gang.

Columbine's Eric Harris and Dylan Klebold also constituted a small-time petty theft gang that had been arrested a year before the Columbine attack. They were also making terrorist threats with explosives. At the time no one thought of the Pearl or Columbine students as gangs, but that is what they were—a group of youths who committed crimes in a group context. We'll look at this in more detail in Chapter 6.

While there had been isolated school attacks in past years, it wasn't a trend. Kids plotting to kill kids and faculty they didn't even know didn't occur with any regularity. The 1997 attack at Pearl High changed that.

The magnitude of the loss of life in Littleton was the reason that Columbine became the trend setter for media notoriety. Twelve students and one teacher were murdered and twenty-one wounded. At Pearl, Luke threatened suicide after the attack. At Columbine, the killers committed suicide to bring an end to their attack. At Pearl and Columbine the teens shot people at random as well as those they knew. The Columbine killers plotted to kill hundreds of students and staff they didn't know, but bombs they planted in the cafeteria never went off.

Like Littleton, Pearl is a wonderful place to live. But oddly, for a period of time, neighborhoods where were worlds apart became sister cities. Since I was one of those superintendents, I quickly learned that leading an educational effort in the middle of such chaos is difficult at best considering all the distractions involved during such a crisis. And like the principal at Columbine, Frank DeAngelis, who has continued to serve at Columbine and live in the community, I did the same. In spite of that terrible day when two of our students died and seven were wounded, my best testimony to the Pearl community is the fact that my wife and I decided to live here when we retired in 2000. We worked in four other communities as educators (my wife was an elementary teacher and later a junior high librarian) before coming to Pearl in 1982. We have no plans at this point to live anywhere else.

There is something about our communities, though, that aggravates students with the Random Actor traits to commit attacks that our inner-city communities seldom ever experience. We will find out what that "something" is in Chapter 8. But for now, let's look at what happened on October 1, 1997.

CHAPTER 3

THE ATTACK

———•———

M ary Anne Woodham rarely allowed her sixteen-year-old son, Luke, to take out the car. He was an inexperienced driver and had poor eyesight. Mrs. Woodham even went so far as to drive him to pick up his occasional dates with his off-and-on girlfriend, Christina Menefee. On the morning of Wednesday October 1, 1997, Luke needed the family car to carry out his plans, and his mother would have stood in the way. According to Luke, his initial plan had been to tie her up and put her in a closet. However, he said he talked to his friend Grant Boyette and Boyette instructed him to kill her.

"So I did," Luke later said. He stabbed his mother seven times. Some of the slash wounds were on her hand and arms, indicating that she had tried to defend herself from the assault. She also had been beaten with a baseball bat that left contusions on her face and body. He then waited with his mother's corpse until it was time for school to begin.

Luke was an above average student but frequently the target of taunting and ridicule from other classmates because of his pudginess, shyness and introverted behavior. Like many other Random Actor students threatening attacks today, he was not a discipline problem in the classroom or on the school campus. He lived alone with his mother at 323 Barrow Street, south of the city center. Mrs. Woodham, who had been divorced five years, worked as a receptionist at a food processing company. She seemed to be a good mother to her two sons. The older son was working and living out of the home at the time of her death. She was said to be over-protective of Luke.

Two things were rumored to have upset Luke Woodham about his home life. First, his father had left the home years earlier in an acrimonious divorce; second, his mother started to date other men. During his trial Luke testified that his mother had "started to party at night." She also inappropriately blamed him for her failed marriage.

After murdering his mother, Luke drove the car to school. First, he went inside before 8:00 a.m. to survey the vast and open commons area where students congregated before classes began. He needed to determine where his targets were standing among the three hundred or so students waiting for the bell to ring.

His other mission upon first entering the commons was to deliver a personal manifesto to his friend Justin Sledge. After leaving the commons he went to his car parked outside in the driveway area.

At 7:55 a.m. he entered the commons for the second time. He was wearing a black overcoat that concealed a 30/06 hunting rifle. Luke then walked up to sixteen-year-old sophomore Christina Menefee, pulled the rifle from his coat and fatally shot her in the lower neck. Methodically, he began moving through the commons, shooting others as students and teachers hid or fled screaming. Lydia Dew, seventeen, was shot in the back.

One of the wounded students, Jerry Safley, later testified that Luke, after shooting him in the commons, said, "I'm sorry Jerry. I didn't mean to shoot you. I thought you were Kyle Foster." By this account, Mayor Jimmy Foster learned that his son Kyle had been a target of the original plan. Investigative work by the local police department revealed that Kyle had been viewed as a high-profile target that would have drawn even greater media attention. But Kyle was stuck in traffic and running late this morning on his way to school.

For the next ten minutes Luke walked around the commons shooting and reloading his rifle. Many shots hit the floor and most of the wounded, other than the two girls killed, were hit from shrapnel as the bullets separated upon contact with the concrete.

Joel Myrick, an officer in a local National Guard unit, and at the time serving as assistant principal of the high school, saw what was happening, sprinted to his truck in the parking lot and retrieved his service .45 automatic pistol. Joel emerged from the faculty parking area around the school and encountered Luke near the driveway where he was attempting to escape from campus. While trying to maneuver in traffic, he lost control of the car and careened into the soft ground that flanked the road. This allowed Joel to stand in front of Luke's car, and, holding his gun on him, command him out of the car. Luke got out of his car and, as Joel placed the gun to his neck, waited until the police arrived to arrest him.

At that point Joel asked Luke why, why, why he had committed such an act? He responded, "Mr. Myrick, the world has wronged me." The police were then on the scene. One officer asked Joel if he could identify the shooter. When Myrick said he didn't know him. Luke, from where he lay on the ground, said, "Oh, you know me, Mr. Myrick. I'm the guy who gave you the discount on the pizza last week."Exactly one week later—when we thought at least the worse was behind us—six more teenagers were arrested in connection with the deadly rampage. They were accused of plotting to help Luke with the attack and the murder of one of the conspirator's fathers. These developments sent panic throughout the Pearl community. The students and faculty, already reeling from the two murders, had to endure the thought that other conspirators, not yet identified, might be in school among them.

The day after the shooting, a student by the name of Justin Sledge moved the already bizarre happening into yet another phase. Justin disrupted a student vigil on campus and attempted to explain to the crowd—who had gathered to pray—why Luke Woodham had committed his act of violence. The students were both frightened and angered by Justin's appearance, feeling he was somehow excusing Luke's actions.

Justin not only disrupted the vigil, he also followed the media around the school campus as if he wanted to make statements to them rationalizing what had happened. That Luke gave Justin his manifesto and other personal papers prior to the shooting confirmed his standing in Luke's hierarchy of friends. Also, Sledge was in the best position to have stopped the shooting, or at least to have warned authorities about Luke's plans.

Earlier in the day, Sledge released to WLBT, a local TV Station, the contents of the notebook that Luke handed him minutes before the shooting. The five-page document contained a self-pitying manifesto that Luke thought would explain why he was committing this violence. In a display of the kind of histrionics that come with adolescence, it also included his last will and testament of his belongings. It summarized his thoughts toward God and his general philosophy of life. The last two pages, which describe the torture and killing of his pet dog, Sparkle, he entitled "My First Kill."

These pages, written in a nearly illegible handwriting, were given to me by a confidential source:

> I am not insane. I am angry. This world shit on me for the final time. I am not spoiled or lazy, for murder is not weak and slow-witted, murder is gutsy and daring. I killed because people like me are mistreated everyday. I do this to show society, "push me and we will push back"! I suffered all my life. No one ever truly loved me. No one ever truly cared about me. I only loved one thing in my whole life and that was Christina Menefee. But she was torn away from me. I tried to save myself with Melissa Williams, but she never cared for

me. As it turns out she made fun of me behind my back while we were together. And all throughout my life I was ridiculed. Always beat on, always hated. Can you, society, truly blame me for what I do? Yes, you will, the ratings wouldn't make good gossip for all the old ladies. But, I shall tell you one thing; I am malicious because I am miserable. The world has turned on me. Wednesday 1, 1997, shall go down in history as the day I fought back. (At this time Grant, say what you will. When you are through, I ask you to read to them sec. 125 of the Gay Science "Madman"). Grant, see you in the holding cell!

Testament of Belongings:
I, Luke Woodham, being of sound mind and body, do hereby will to Grant Boyette my books. To Lucas Thompson, my guitars and amplifiers and their equipment. Also all of my guitar magazines and guitar books. I leave my music and lyrics to Lucas Thompson, so that he may perform. I also leave my other writings of philosophy and poetry to Grant Boyette, they are parts of me and must be published as a piece of my life. Also, to Grant Boyette I will all my cassette tapes.

God and Philosophy:
They are able! I am hatred in every man's heart! I am the epitome of all evil! I have no mercy for humanity, for they created me, they tortured me until I snapped and became what I am today! My advice to any man that has been tortured by humanity is this: Let these words ring throughout your heart, mind and soul! Hate humanity! Hate humanity's way! Hate what humanity has made you! Hate what you have become! Most of all hate the accursed God of Christianity. Hate him for making humanity! Hate him for making you! Hate him

for flinging you into a monstrous life you did not ask for nor deserve! Fill your heart, mind, and soul with hatred, until it's all you know. Until your conscience becomes a fiery tomb of hatred for the goodness in your soul. Hate everyone and everything. Hate what you were and are. Hate until you can't anymore. Then learn, read poetry, books, philosophy books, history books, science books, autobiographies and biographies. Become a sponge for knowledge. Study the philosophies of others and condense the parts you like as your own. Make your own rules, live by your own laws. For now, truly, you should be at peace and your own true self. Live your life in a bold new way. For you dear friend are a superman.

My First Kill:
4-14-97 on Saturday of last week, I made my first kill. The date was April 12, 1997, about 4:30 p.m. The victim was a loved one. My dear dog Sparkle. Me and an accomplice had been beating the bitch for a while and last Tuesday I took a day off from school just because I didn't want to go. My friend came over and we beat the dog. I was afraid the vet my brother had wanted to call would notice all the bruises on the dog and I would get in trouble. So, I called my accomplice and he came over. We beat the dog, and laid her upon a plastic garbage bag. We put the subdued little bitch in an old book bag and went to some woods. When we got out to the woods I took a billy club that I had and handed it to my accomplice. He ran and hit the bagged dog with it. I will never forget the howl she made, it sounded almost human. We laughed and hit her hard. We drug her across the ground deeper into the woods. We opened the book bag, tore a hole in the bag and brought her top half out. We kicked a nearby

THE ATTACK / 27

ant bed and let them bite her. We put the plastic bags to the side where we later burned them. We placed the dog in the book bag and went further into the woods. When we reached a clean area, I pulled out my lighter and lighter fluid, made a trail with the fluid, across the grass and into the book bag and lit it. The bag burned some. We put more fluid on there and we heard the dog scream. A hole developed in the bag and the dog stuck her head out, fully engulfed in flames. We put more on her, and more and more and more. She got out of the bag and tried to run. I took the nightstick and hit her in the shoulder, spine and neck. I'll never forget the sound her bones made breaking under my might. We set her on fire again, the foolish dog opened her mouth and we sprayed fluid down her throat, her whole neck caught on fire, inside and out. Finally the fire went out and she was making a gurgling noise. I silenced the noise with the club again. I hit her so hard crushed burned skin on her shoulder fell off. I hit so hard I knocked the fur off her neck. Then we put her in the burned bag and chunked her in a nearby pond. We watched the bag sink. It was true beauty.

Before I made a copy of these writings, I sat in the easy chair in my living room and tried to make sense of what this deeply disturbed young man had written. I wished we had been able to find out about his tormented feelings and had helped him and in turn prevented this tragedy.

Of the six teens arrested as conspirators, five were current students at Pearl High School. The sixth was attending classes at Hinds Community College. Pearl Police Chief Bill Slade said charges brought against all six stemmed from the shooting attack. Two of the suspects were charged with a second conspiracy to commit murder for planning to kill Donald Brooks, Sr., the father of one of the suspects.

Three of the conspirators were arrested Monday night, October 6. They were Marshall "Grant" Boyette, Jr., 18; Donald P. Brooks II, 17; and Justin Sledge, 16. The other three suspects were arrested Tuesday morning at Pearl High School and led from the school in handcuffs. Those students were Wesley Brownell, 17; Daniel "Lucas" Thompson, 16; and Delbert "Allen" Shaw, 18.

Luke Woodham—as announced by Chief Slade—was charged with three counts of murder and seven counts of aggravated assault.

According to investigators, the seven youths, including Woodham, had been discussing an attack on the school since the beginning of the year. They often met at Woodham's house since his mother was usually at work. After attacks on the school, they intended to escape to Louisiana, then Mexico, and finally to Cuba. These meetings were a confused mix of mythology, philosophy, poetry, and religion. The boys were above average students and in most cases self-proclaimed intellectuals and thinkers. They gathered philosophical writings and incorporated half-understood passages in their own kind of ethos. The indictments also pointed to their goals to acquire power and large amounts of money.

The investigators soon determined that Grant Boyette, the college student, was the leader of the group. The *Clarion Ledger* ran a story naming Boyette as the accomplice in the killing of Luke's pet dog. Grant's father was a military recruiter and his mother a star teacher in one of our elementary schools. The family had deep spiritual roots in the local Southern Baptist Church and were respected members of the community.

Boyette took particular interest in the works of Friedrich Nietzsche. He was drawn to the nihilism and the questioning of morality he found there. Another Boyette hero was Adolph Hitler; he claimed to admire the way Hitler influenced people in his rise to absolute power.

A second person in the hierarchy of leadership in the group was Justin Sledge. He had received Luke's manifesto and was in the best position to have prevented the violent tragedy. In his senior year, while attending his Accelerated English III Class, Justin wrote a paper titled "Who Am I." He divided his paper into three parts: "Who Am I?"; "Where Have I Been?"; and "Where Am I Going?" Sledge stated in the first section, "I practice the ancient pseudo science of alchemy and find myself a scholar of philosophy and natural science. Sadly, in all my learning I have forsaken the most basic of all human gifts, compassion. My heart is like a dark, cold night that never ends. I wish to one-day find love in something if not somebody. I must be realistic; who would love such a learned wretch? When people comment, I wish I were as smart as you, I wish I could tell them of the massive sacrifice I have made for my mentality."

The teacher, after correcting numerous minor errors, complimented him on his command of language. She also wrote in the margin, "Much of this I do not understand."

Did his paper suggest faults in his overall mental ability, or did it point to his brilliance and future as a scholar? At the time, I would have told you the assessment well could be in the eyes of the beholder. Now I know these are the writings of a severely troubled student who had the Random Actor traits.

Sledge, speaking for Luke, insisted that Luke's actions were not the result of a "boyfriend-girlfriend thing," nor were they a consequence of Luke's parents' divorce. In attempting to elevate Luke's motives, Sledge claimed Luke was responding to a society that had put him down. Sledge told the *Clarion Ledger* reporters present, "We as a society must change." The reality was that problems at home did affect who Luke became and the rest was a context in which to act out his rage.

Luke resented the way athletics and social achievements were valued above academics. Justin and his group felt academics were their strength. But local society dealt the thinkers a bad hand, Sledge told newspaper and TV station reporters at the vigil. Paranoia was clearly at hand in these rantings.

It is noteworthy that the manifesto did not refer to Satan or devil worship. Rumors of satanism had run rampant through our shell-shocked community the week after the incident. However, Sledge's hint—after explaining Luke's actions—that the violence might not be over sent the community into a full-scale panic. His arrest—along with other conspirators—was a decision made by the county district attorney and the Pearl Police Department and was heartily welcomed by the majority of the citizens.

The press tried to connect the group to satanic worship; however, very little of substance came out concerning this implication. Investigators mentioned only that Boyette had prayed to Satan in group meetings. Korem says it's common for Random Actors who kill to spiritualize their rage. He said this is present in about 80 percent of Random Actor killers. They use the spiritual twist to inflate their importance and minimize their paranoia. Hitler and Saddam Hussein did it, as have other student killers. It's from this platform that they *drive an I'm more powerful than you* dogma."[1] Hitler, for example, had all references to Jews removed from the Bible as he ascended to power, and the Nazi cabinet almost resigned in protest in 1933. In 1998, Saddam had pints of his blood extracted from his body and used it to write "a handwritten copy of the Koran—over 6,000 verses and 336,000 words—in appreciation of being delivered from many 'conspiracies and dangers'."[2]

How much Boyette actually dabbled with satanic themes is open to debate. He was, however, fixated on Nietzsche, as seen through his references to "Madman" and "Superman," and his use of Nietzsche-

THE ATTACK / 31

like imperative sentences and exclamation points. According to Nietzsche, a Madman is someone who is truly enlightened but whom society views as insane. A Madman, metaphorically, is the one to rush out in broad daylight, holding a lantern in his hand. As Dr. James Bartlett, professor emeritus of modern languages at the University of Mississippi, puts it, Nietzsche's Superman "will go around society and say, God is dead. God had to die because he was the cosmic peeping tom."

Never forget, Bartlett emphasizes, that the Nazis also started with Nietzsche's philosophy, twisted it to their needs, and ended up killing six million Jews. If a whole nation could fall victim to that type of misinterpretation, an adolescent such as Luke certainly could be vulnerable. Many scholars believe that Nietzsche's poetic work is open to almost any interpretation.

In giving further analysis of the manifesto, Reverend Don Malin of Clinton, Mississippi, said the statement "We will push back" clearly referred to a group. "They all feel like they've been mistreated so they identify with Nietzsche by being the anti-hero. A group of people can find the strength to do things that an individual may or may not do."

Dan Korem's Random Actor profile is a perfect fit for these paranoid and bizarre themes (more in Chapter 8). Violent offenders have a long history of perverting and misappropriating literature, of finding personal messages within a text, and of searching out literature that can be fitted to their own individual philosophies. *The Turner Diaries*, a fictional story of white victory in a global race war, written by neo-Nazi William Pierce, was integral to the worldview of Timothy McVeigh—who blew up the federal building in Oklahoma City in 1995, killing 168 and injuring more than 500. He reportedly carried around a copy of the book and tried to get his Army buddies to read it. *The Turner Diaries* became the blueprints for the white supremacist group known as the Order.

Mark David Chapman's obsessive and schizophrenic reading of J.D. Salinger's *The Catcher in the Rye* inspired his assassination of John Lennon. In a delusional blurring of reality and entertainment, John Hinkley decided to shoot President Ronald Reagan in an effort to impress actress Jody Foster after watching her role in Martin Scorseses's movie *Taxi Driver.*

The murders and arrests in Pearl placed the national spotlight on our community. *NBC Nightly News* called the events a "Shocker in a small town." *CBS Morning News*, *CNN*, and *ABC* covered the murders and the additional arrests. Local, national, and international newspapers were on site covering the incident and its related stories.

When the media vans departed, they left behind a community still bewildered. The national media continued to cover the story relentlessly until I with board approval stopped the frenzy by declaring Pearl High School off limits to the media on the third day after the incident. Media contact was provided through the district central office. We couldn't reestablish academic structure in school until we were relieved from the relentless media contact.

The shock to our community continued after the additional teenagers were arrested. The high point of alarm was when police escorted three accused student conspirators from the high school in handcuffs. Across America, the incident continued to be breaking news. But in Pearl, everyone wanted to know what was going to happen next and when would it all end? Every parent phone call repeatedly asked, "Is it safe to send my child to school?"

CHAPTER 4

THE MONSTER
IN THE HALLWAY

JOEL A. MYRICK, ASSISTANT PRINCIPAL

———◆———

J oel Myrick was the assistant principal the day of the attack. In his own words, he conveys his raw visceral account of what he experienced moment by moment the day of the attack and how he apprehended Luke before he could kill again. Had he not acted and put his life in harm's way, it's likely that many more may have been killed and wounded.

The Commons. Last year, it was decorated as a medieval castle. Our Madrigal Singers harmonized in their best English accent. The sixty-foot high hard walls spread their symphony through the echoes of space.

The day of the attack as I walk through the pre-school gatherings, the blended voices of hundreds of teenagers echo. A cup of coffee in hand, I move through the crowd towards my office, mentally ticking off the day's duties as the assistant principal.

As I approach the door to my office area which opens to the Commons, a loud, echoing boom resounds from somewhere behind me, then silence. As I turn, a second explosion sounds, then another.

As the reverberations fade, they are replaced by a building crescendo of wailing, screaming voices. No words, just the frantic sounds of terror, growing, multiplying in pitch and volume. *What in the world?*

Within seconds, the reality of the source of the sound is clear . . . gun . . . a big gun. *My God.*

Dozens of young people from the immediate area flood toward me. I step aside . . . the door is open. The office area quickly fills. Throughout the initial chaos, my eyes remain transfixed in the directions of the gunfire. Now stepping quickly, cautiously towards the corner of the stairwell, the only fixture obscuring my complete vision of the vast common area, I search for the unseen . . . the unbelievable source of my being is on fire, on the edge, fearfully searching.

Another loud boom, cement and cinder block fly though the air as the bullet smashes into a three by three foot column in the center of the Commons. A young Indian girl screams, twists in pain, falls to the cold tile floor. *Stop*, I say in my mind as my vision narrows to a tunnel surrounded by a grey fog. *Move*, I tell myself but my body cannot, paralyzed. I stand aghast, living in a liquid-like dream of horror.

The tip of the rifle appears first, a shocking processional to the monster to follow. Walking confidently, without peer, the large creature moves towards and past its latest victim. The lever-action rifle at the hip, the devil's head sweeps slowly back and forth, scanning the area, soaking in the pain. The power of death flows from its eyes . . . insanity. The red face, flushed with hot blood, radiates evil. A plume of hot, diffracted vapor, trails upward and back behind its head.

Three young students huddle behind one of the four large columns. Smelling their fear, it walks toward them. I cannot believe what I am seeing. One young man steps out from behind the columns protection, raising his book bag to shield his chest. He screams, "No man, NO!"

The beast adjusts its aim, pointing to the center of the boy's belly. The thunder of the rifle knocks the boy to the ground, a red mist of blood and guts spray out and downward behind him. The other two kids, a boy and a girl, run away. The muzzle of the rifle follows, firing low and behind them, splattering them with shards of tile and lead. They both go down next to the wall.

For the first time since the first shot, like a burst of light, I realize what is happening . . . the kids are being killed . . . they are dying. My mind and sight shift, I see everything at once. Everything is clear. The monster turns away. I see it thumbing more cartridges into the rifle's tubular magazine. What do I do? To rush across the Commons, some thirty of forty steps, would be insane. If he turns, there will be nowhere to hide, no cover. I feel trapped, trapped by my fear, trapped by my horror. Staring at the back of the thing, watching the gun, thinking of how to stop it, the solution is clear . . . get my gun.

I run towards the exit, across the Common's expanse, my legs moving on their own. I am moving without touching the floor . . . seemingly ten feet above it . . . flying . . . too slowly. Halfway across, I turn and look, the scene forever frozen in my mind . . . the smell of gun smoke . . . silence. I see the creature walking away, the sinister silhouette backlit by the ethereal glow of the science hall where I used to teach physics . . . dark and foreboding. Bodies are sprawled in non-peaceful poses. I see Ms. Safely, the health teacher standing beside two injured students looking down . . . she seems . . . so bizarre . . . to be in casual conversation. I turn back to the path of my truck . . . refocusing on getting something . . . to help . . . to make this nightmare stop.

Bursting out of the double-doors at the rear of the school, I simultaneously reach for the encased gun in my truck. I place it on the seat while unzipping the canvas case. A Colt .45 automatic, an Officer's Model . . . and cold . . . rests in the soft fleece.

The gun is familiar. As a National Guard combat unit commander . . . an artilleryman . . . I carry a pistol in the field. I keep it close off duty, firing it often in training, to protect against "enemies, foreign and domestic." All this bravado . . . this past patriotic posturing . . . quickly disappears as I lift the pistol, pointing the barrel skyward, wrapping my other hand around the weapon, ready to load a round into the chamber.

At that moment, I forget why I am doing what I am doing. All I can think is *I am loading my gun on school property.* The act so foreign, so incredibly wrong, guns/school . . . like placing a hand in the fire, I never do this. The decision already made, I load the gun, flip on the safety, and turn back, towards the school, back towards the bad dream.

As I turn, I see a face, clear, brown eyes looking at me uncertainly. A custodian, an older black woman, stands at the cafeteria loading-door . . . one foot in, one foot out . . . prepared to run away regardless of the direction. She must have known what was unfolding inside. I pause in mid-step, my eyes meeting hers. She simply says, "Oh my." I continue on my way, strangely comforted . . . encouraged by the eyes of another.

My instinctive plan is to flank the enemy. The killer may have seen me running across the Commons . . . it may be following me now. I must see it first . . . take it by surprise. My mental calculations stem more from childhood games of "kick-the-can" than any formal military training. As a boy, my neighborhood friends played the game nightly in the summertime, around the elementary school. One person stood in close proximity to an empty soda can while the rest of the kids attempted to sneak up and kick the can, thus winning. If you were spotted in your attempt, the kid who was "it" kicked the can and you were dead. Simple rules . . . kick the can . . . don't get caught. No longer running wildly, I move deliberately, focused, in a now deadly version of the game in my childhood memory.

I move around the side of the school towards the front doors, the opposite of my original position. As I round the final corner before the entrance, I see students scattered around the area . . . some in cars, others standing still in pods or alone. The glitter of dew on the grass is a star-like backdrop to the frozen constellations of human forms. The four lanes of the interstate highway are two hundred yards away. The cars and trucks fly by, a moving backdrop, oblivious to the chaos occurring such a short distance away on such a beautiful morning, October 1, 1997.

As I approach the school's front doors, thirty strides away, again, the gun barrel appears . . . reeling me back to the bad dream. As the bow of a ship, parting the waves, the blue-black steel dividing the doors brings me back to the life and death moment I am living. Oddly, I am reminded of old film footage of an alleged "Bigfoot" monster as the rifle bearing creature walks with long, slow strides out of the Commons to the East into the morning sun . . . slowly pivoting its head.

Immediately, I slide to a halt . . . a frozen memorial, gripping the pistol with both hands and shout, "Stop!" The animal . . . man turns his head, never breaking stride and looks me in the eyes. Wearing wire-rimmed glasses. The hair is medium length and tousled. A thigh-length coat hides the belt and pockets. He seems perturbed by my presence, although he seems to acknowledge mine. I never take my weapon off safe because there are students everywhere. Again, I feel as if things are moving in slow motion, as if the immediate presence of the rifle slows time, a clear and present danger warping my sense of perception.

Unnoticed until now, an empty white car sits awkwardly to my left at the end of the walkway . . . the passenger's side tires up on the sidewalk. The killer walks around the rear of the car and opens the driver's side door. I don't realize I am moving, just drifting forward . . . no sound, just sight . . . magnified, clear at the focal point . . .

blurred at the edges. When he slams the car door shut, I snap out of the fog, realizing he is leaving. There is one path to escape. Fifty yard ahead of him to the south is a stop sign. A right turn leads west, curving northward to Highway 80 that runs east and west, west towards the elementary school where my son and other children now sit in a classroom, unaware of the evil loose in our part of the world.

As I run forward, parallel to the car's path, I see the rear wheel smoking . . . moving away. He guns the motor toward the stop sign where another car sits, waiting its turn, oblivious to the death in the rear view mirror. Impatiently, the shooter stops, blows his horn, backs up . . . ready to pass the stopped car. The interference gives me enough time to run thirty yards to a road-side position twenty yards to the west of the stop sign. My mind is racing. *He cannot leave.* I know he must pass this position. I must stop him. I am not sure how, I only know for certain that I have a pistol in my hand. I don't know if and where I will shoot . . . tires, door, or head. I was taught, "If you pull your weapon, be prepared to use it or don't pull it at all." I stand on the edge of the road, weapon off safe and pointed skyward, finger on the trigger, standing on the brink of a previous impossibility.

Wheeling around the stopped car, the killer turns, toward me. I raise the pistol, subconsciously scanning the backdrop of the interstate's roadbed, where stray bullets might fly. He sees me standing there. He swerves off the road, away from me, attempting to create as much space between us as possible. In the damp grass of the road's shoulder, the car loses traction, spinning to a stop, the car is facing . . . the monster is facing me at ten steps. His hands are on the top of the steering wheel. His glasses sit askew on his nose, one side lower than the other. An insane countenance radiates from his face. I am looking at the devil.

My pistol is aimed at his face . . . those horrible eyes . . . surely insanity resides within.

"Don't move or I'll blow your head off."

I just say this . . . no thought or premeditation . . . simply the strongest statement possible. No further instructions were required.

His hands remain visible as I step side ways to the driver's window, never taking my eyes off the gun sights silhouetted by his face. I can see black electrical tape around his hands, and the rifle, muzzle down, leaning on the seat beside him. His breathing is exaggerated, short and heaving, as if he were about to explode. As I reach down with my left hand, opening the door, the muzzle of my pistol is two feet from his head. At that moment, a metamorphosis occurs. His face changes shape and color. He changes size, Jekyll and Hyde. The swollen madman exorcises into a chubby adolescent. I immediately feel odd, almost ashamed for holding a gun to his head.

I direct him out of the car onto the ground. He lies on his stomach. I pull his coat over his head, exposing his soft white back. I look for more weapons. Finding none, I ask him, "Why . . . Why . . . Why are you killing my kids?"

He turns his head slightly out of the grass and says "The world has wronged me and I couldn't take it anymore."

I respond without thinking. "Wait till you get to Parchman Penitentiary."

To my left I hear tires sliding on gravel. A police car comes to a stop. Out steps another officer, gun drawn. He asks, "Is that the shooter?"

"Yes, this is the shooter."

"Who is it?" he asks.

"I don't know," I replied.

The young man on the ground turns again and says in a calm, almost hurt tone, "Oh, you know me, Mr. Myrick. I'm the guy who gave you the discount on the pizza last week."

I stand there pulverized by the emotional onslaught I have endured in the last few minutes: Horror, fear, uncertainty, pity, and shame.

I look at the sky, all the emotions boil out. I scream . . . groan, the emotions taking audible form. "AHHHH."

My head bows again to the spectacle on the ground. I ask the officer, "You got him?"

Gun drawn, the officer replies, "I got him."

The cop looks at me . . . unsure on what to do about a distraught civilian carrying a .45 automatic, walking away . . . leaving him with a young man on the ground.

Walking to the edge of the road, I kneel down, clear my weapon, stand up and slide the pistol under my belt. I walk two or three steps slowly picking up speed . . . running back to the school.

Entering the front door, the door the shooter had exited, I can still smell the burnt powder. The students and teachers, who have not fled the building, remain hidden away . . . behind closed doors . . . in horror . . . waiting.

Once again the fog sets in. I can only see one victim at a time . . . everything else is blurred.

I walk up to a young girl lying on her back, long brown hair matted in a pool of blood around her head and neck. I can see a wound low, on her throat. I bend down and touch her neck, checking for a pulse. She is warm. She isn't moving. No pulse. I cannot sense any life. I pray out loud, "God bless this child. God bless this child."

I turn. A few feet away lay a curly-haired girl . . . Lydia. I know her. She is dropped off at school early every day. Normally she sits on the floor of the Commons, often by herself, and says "Good Morning," without fail. Her eyes are now fluttering. She has been shot in the side. Blood soaks her clothes. I straddle her body, bending down, staring at her face. Her eyes stop fluttering, remaining open. She is looking at me with a surprised, yet peaceful gaze. No movement. She is gone. I touch her side and lift my hand in front of my face . . . bright red blood. I pray out loud, "God bless this child. God bless this child".

I stand up. A teacher, Ms. Duckworth, appears beside me. She holds Lydia . . . a mother's touch. An EMT and police officer are making their way across the Commons. They are saying something. I cannot hear a thing.

The Commons are coming alive. People are moving in the halls, classrooms, and offices. Everyone is a blur. I see a popular history teacher, Mr. Sansing, walking towards me. His white shirt and tie seemingly out of place. His white hair combed back, framing a face of bewilderment and shock. He is saying something, but I cannot hear it.

I walk a few more steps. I can see the young man who has been shot in the belly with someone crouched over him. I walk . . . stagger, I see a trail of blood on the white tiles. Mindlessly, I begin to follow the trail. It leads along the path I had previously taken to my truck. I didn't notice the blood before . . . maybe it was made afterwards. I follow, looking down . . . tiny drops . . . sprayed blood. The trail leads out of the building towards the band hall. I enter the hall and find dozens of students, huddled, weeping, holding one another. The blood trail ends with a blonde haired young man with a bloody leg wound. The band director's face reflects disbelief.

I walk out of the band hall, wandering, empty, and spent. I circle the football dressing room and look across the manicured playing field . . . oddly comforting in its green perfection. The field house door opens and Coach Merchant walks toward me. "What in the world happened?"

I relay the terrible moments. Then, I tell coach, "I got him."

"Good," he says.

We sit together for a few minutes on the wooden porch, sirens in the background. The world changed today.

Alone, uncounted time drifts by, I wander back towards the school, a huge brick complex, modeled after a cathedral. The east and west entrances tower skyward, the dark glass converging, pointing to the morning sky. State Troopers are now there . . . in the wood line surrounding the school, a picket line of sorts . . . defending against . . . for what had never entered my mind . . . others.

On the west side of the high school a crowd has begun to gather, held back by the police. They stand . . . I can see a group of grown-ups . . . parents and some children . . . dozens of indistinguishable bodies . . . pressing to advance. As I come closer, one face becomes clear. Ms. Long, the mother of Lydia, took shape. She is an acquaintance of sorts . . . the mother of one of my children, one of my students.

I am numb to everything . . . feelings, fatigue . . . no emotion left. I walk toward the line. I scan the crowd but my eyes return to Ms. Long. Her eyes are locked on mine . . . a magnet. I am drawn to those eyes. I approach the line. Without words, her hand grasps mine . . . I turn and lead her back to the school. She says things but I am without comprehension. We walk . . . I lead . . . unable to meet her eyes again. I will take her to her baby. As we approach the entry, the same teacher who had shared with me the moment of Lydia's death takes Ms. Long's hand from mine and leads her away. I stop. I do not know why the teacher took Lydia's mom away, I watch as they hold one another. Mothers' eyes must have met—through which the news of Lydia's passing must have been told.

I enter the Commons again. It is a beehive of activity and the faint smell of gunpowder lingers, reminding me of the horrible minutes before. Public and school officials stand in assorted groups, pondering the scene.

In, I walk past the groups, not wanting to speak. Their eyes meet mine, attempting to draw me over, but no one speaks aloud . . . only whispering to each other as I continue my mindless path. As I approach the dead girls, their head and shoulders framed by their own blood, I can see the occasional brass cartridge strewn about the area. No one turns me away. I look up to see a photographer leaning over the balcony above the girls, creating images, flashing the children as lightning from the sky. I look down once more. Book bags are scattered about like bales of hay in the field. The girls, laid awkwardly, urine soaked jeans, seemed so undignified. I want to wake them up and send them to their homes, away from the eyes of these strangers. Teenage girls . . . they would be so embarrassed to be seen in such a state.

As I stare, recording the scene, I see flies . . . flies lighting on the dead girls. Indignant, I quickly remove my coat, stepping closer, waving the coat, shooing the flies away. This is now my purpose in life . . . to keep the flies away. A police officer, standing guard over the scene, quickly looks down and away, embarrassed for me and for them, not knowing what he should do. The blood is separating, a mixture of dark and clear . . . and the flies, not knowing the holy nature of their food. I continue to fan the flies away, careful not to touch anything but the air. I continue my vigil for an undetermined time until suddenly, realizing the scene I must be creating, stop and walk away . . . oddly embarrassed, ashamed . . . so alone in the presence of so many. I put on my coat. I feel the gun stuck in the waistline of my pants. I walk out of the school to my truck, where I return my pistol to its original location.

Walking around the school, following the path I had taken before, I see the teachers being gathered, herded into a school bus. I ask what is going on. They strangely detach from everyone else. The bus begins to pull away. The eyes of the teachers look down at me . . . revealing a shocked pity. I turn back and walk back into the school.

Returning to the Commons, I see Mr. Arnold, the assistant superintendent, a tall, slender man in his sixties. Our eyes meet and we walk towards one another.

"He shot them . . . I saw him . . . I got my gun and got him," I explained.

"I know, Mr. Myrick. This is a terrible thing. God bless you," he replies.

I turn and am approached by a plain-clothed policeman and two other men. He tells them, "This is Mr. Myrick. He apprehended the shooter." He shakes my hand. I feel strange, yet comforted to be, at last, a part of everyone else.

Remembering my family, I walk to my office and first call the elementary where my son attends. Someone answers the phone and I tell her to tell Elijah Myrick that his daddy is OK. She says she would, but she sounds confused by the odd request. Second, I call my wife, leaving a message. Then I call my father, the chief administrator for the City of Laurel, quickly tell him what has happened, and that I am fine. Hanging up, I walk back out to the Commons. The police have placed a sheet over each girl and taped off the area. I wonder why they do not just take them away.

An officer approaches as I exit the office, he asks if I will go down to the station and make a statement. I agree and walk to my truck. Driving out of the parking lot and up the school road to the highway, I pass dozens of police and media groups. When I reach the highway, the police wave me through. As I turn onto the highway a rush of relief washes over me. I am away . . . among the normal . . . a thirty-five-year-old man in his truck accelerating away . . . a nightmare fading into the rearview mirror.

An officer stands post at the entrance to the police parking lot. He stops me, then recognizing me, he waves me through. I pull into a space and walk into the station. I tell the receptionist my business. She directs me down a hall where a detective reaches for the doorknob, another detective tells him the shooter is there. He quickly turns away and leads me to the next room, which is open. I feel a strange desire to go back to the other room and question the "shooter." Our proximity is strange. I can feel him through the walls. The young detective, Aaron Hirschfield, introduces himself and asks me to write down what has happened. I sit at an old desk and recount the bizarre events of the morning. I feel out of place, like

I am remembering a movie. I try to sequence everything.

Completing and signing the statement, I feel relieved and want to go back to school. After reading the statement, the detective shakes my hand and says I am a hero. His look of admiration is tempered by the same odd pity that seems to be on everyone's face. I don't feel like a hero. I feel like I did my job . . . like breaking up a fight or picking up a dropped book for a student. I return to my truck and drive back to Pearl High School.

Entering the parking lot after passing through a gauntlet of check points, each one giving the same strange look, I see a huge satellite truck sitting outside the school. I wonder why. Passing the truck, a reporter sees me, looking curious; she begins to move in the direction of my moving truck. I speed up, rounding the school and park in my usual place. The reporter is walking quickly in my direction. I hop out of the truck and quickly make my way to the door. It is locked. I quickly fumble for my key, barely making my way inside as the reporter calls my name.

Entering the Commons, I see the bodies have been removed and inmates from the local jail are mopping up the blood. They seem ashamed of their task . . . I am embarrassed for them. I want to help them . . . this is my job. I want to finish my job, at which I have failed . . . taking care of the girls. I stand alone in the middle of the great hall, superimposing the image of the dead and wounded on the now empty Commons floor. I have nothing to do. Again I am alone, and I suddenly feel an enormous sense of loss and sorrow. I want to go home.

An officer appears, talking on the radio, he tells me I am needed at the school district's central office. There is a meeting. I wonder what the agenda will be . . . will I have to tell the story again? I am still dazed.

Nothing makes sense other than the need to wake up from this nightmare and see all the kids going about their normal school day. I turn again and begin making my way back to the truck, peeking out of the doors before walking swiftly to the truck, wanting to avoid the media. I drive a wide arc around the satellite truck. Speeding away as the reporters point toward me, talking excitedly. The feeling of relief again washes over me as I pass the last roadblock.

Turning onto the highway, toward the central office and the meeting, I try to guess what the conversation will be. Students were shot dead in the school by another student . . . period. I can't believe others would want to discuss it . . . rehash it. The parking lot is packed. I look for a spot and end up parking on the shoulder of the highway. Shock and fatigue are taking their toll. My legs are wobbly, my eyes tired, my head hurts. I enter the building where people, mostly strangers, are standing and sitting in small groups, whispering. Some see me walk in and stare or turn to the others, directing their attention to me. I feel embarrassed, then outraged. I think, *Give me a break. Go Away.*

The superintendent, Dr. William Dodson, a stately, older gentlemen, comes to me and leads me to his office. The school board attorney, Skip Jernigan is sitting down, a strained look on his face. Dr. Dodson begins by stating that a young man, a student, had killed two students and wounded seven others. He goes on to say that the boy had killed his mother before coming to the school.

"I am glad you were there, Mr. Myrick."

I am sick upon learning the number of students involved. I hadn't known the full events of the day, never comprehended the boy on the ground could have killed his mother too. Mr. Jernigan says this is becoming a national news event and the district needs to have a plan on how to handle it and how and when to return to school. I appreciate the order, the coolness in which the men carried on. Surely they will help my head to clear . . . to return to the happy man I was earlier this morning.

The meeting is stiff: The reporters ask questions, the authorities recite the facts, and I . . . my mind, swims in a pool—a foggy pool of nothingness. I am too tired to relate, to really care.

As I leave the office, driving back down the highway past the high school entrance, I stop at the red light. I look to my right; the brick, Pearl High sign has become a memorial, testimony, a tombstone covered with candles and notes from students. A vigil of sorts is taking place. I see students, parents, and others gathering, trying to make sense of the day. I return home, I walk into the house. Patty, my wife, comes to me and holds me. My legs are weak. She slides a kitchen chair behind me. I sit down. Tears fill my eyes. This day, a day that changed the world, is done.

CHAPTER 5

A PERSONAL DEBRIEF

———•———

At the start of my administrative career in 1970, I was employed as an assistant principal in a racially mixed inner-city high school in the Mississippi Delta. My duties consisted of breaking up fights, mediating student conflicts, resolving problems from student walkouts and meeting with angry parents. There were frequent court appearances, time spent on the witness stand, and other civil rights related matters. Witness duty was distasteful; witnesses stayed in an isolated room all during the trial until called to testify. The clash between the races seldom became violent, but there were always tensions that we constantly tried to resolve.

No one ever told me that school administration would be easy, and I never expected it to be. I was told it would offer challenges and its share of problems, but that personal satisfaction and the opportunity to make a positive difference in the lives of America's youth were both the rewards and the compelling reasons to pursue an education career. My three decades of experiences have brought me so much more of both elements than I ever imagined. The rewards have far exceeded my expectations, but I must confess the challenges have been overwhelming at times.

When Luke Woodham unexpectedly attacked our school near the end of my career, he brought the beginning of my career forcefully to mind. Up until that day, the tumultuous civil rights problems and injustices of the 1970's seemed about as difficult and ominous as anything I would ever be called upon to handle. The October 1, 1997, attack, though, made the earlier period seem like a quiet day at the office.

Although I didn't personally know Luke, I couldn't fathom why he would bring his hunting rifle to school concealed under his coat and open fire. As a boy, I would hear my parents talk about Pearl Harbor Day, December 7, a day that would live in infamy. In Pearl, we all seem to mark the day of the attack with October 1, 1997. Sort of like it was the day Random Actor school attacks invaded American schools. We're not obsessed with it, just marked by it.

Students were gathered in the Commons, as they did every morning, awaiting the beginning of classes. Luke deliberately shot at point blank range the student he had already chosen to kill. It's terrible, but we can at least understand that he irrationally focused on and killed a girl who didn't want to be his girlfriend. *But why all the rest?* He fired indiscriminately, wounding seven more students as they lunged for cover where there was none. At the end of his ten-minute shooting spree, two students died, and seven were wounded.

This is my short personal debrief of that day:

I was already in my office, studying my calendar and making coffee, when all the morning quietness halted. Oscar Moore, my transportation director, burst into my office and said, "Doctor Dodson, we gotta get over to the high school now."

The tone of his voice made me hurry to scramble into his maintenance truck. We shot away, uncharacteristically toward Pearl High School.

"It's bad, isn't it?" I asked.

Oscar was shaking his head as he gripped the wheel until his knuckles looked like old piano keys.

"The worst," he said. He struggled with the next words.

"It's a shooter, bunch of students down."

"You mean dead," I finished. He nodded.

All the school shootings I had ever heard about flashed through my mind. I searched for possible motives.

"Was it a love triangle?" I suggested only half out loud. I had never been involved in a school shooting, though down through the years a handful of students had attempted to bring weapons to school. I'd also been involved in student suicide attempts, but they had always occurred off campus and most of them had fortunately been unsuccessful.

Clearly, I was trying to rationally summon some experience, any experience that would help me deal with a tragedy of this proportion. I concluded that this incident was well outside of my experience as a superintendent.

Pirate Cove, the dead end street leading directly to the school, was already filled with curious citizens, law enforcement personnel and flashing emergency vehicles. Our movement slowed to a crawl.

"Get off the road, use the drainage ditch," I instructed Oscar, nodding toward the long concrete culvert leading directly along the street to the school. And down we went.

As we flew along the drainage ditch, I spotted Pearl Police, Rankin County Deputies, and Mississippi Highway Patrol. All had weapons drawn positioning themselves hurriedly around the grounds. Over seventy officers from surrounding jurisdictions responded within minutes of the shooting. My whole career began to reel before me and I was glad I had learned one lesson well: regardless of what I faced inside the school this morning, I had to meet it head-on, with all my ability.

The greenery of the school lawn presented a lovely backdrop to the school setting, still quiet on this beautiful fall morning. Finally, Oscar's truck bumped to an abrupt stop about twenty feet from the main school entrance, and we were both running for the door. My first sight was deserted book bags scattered around the gray tile floor in the Commons area.

The smell of gunpowder was overwhelming as we crunched over the bright red shell casings that littered the tiles between the book bags. The concrete columns, which led up to an atrium ceiling, were pock marked with bullet holes like a gang war scene on a TV episode. Yellow crime scene tape corralled the lot; a few loose ends of clothing and paper fluttered as if a strong breeze had created the scene. Slowed to a walk, I spotted a few teachers and emergency personnel bent over a number of downed students. They appeared to have recently emerged from the guidance office on my right.

I saw John Craven, one of our assistant principals, get up from his knees, wipe his hands on his back hip pockets and begin to walk heavily almost as if wading through water toward me.

"They need you in the counselor's office," he said. His face drained of blood.

I was three steps from the entrance to the guidance office. I found myself unprepared for what I saw. Two bodies were literally at my feet.

A light green hospital sheet lay loosely scattered over what had to be a body. I nodded, and John knelt and lifted the sheet maybe eight or ten inches up from the head. The fallen female had turned blue, but there was no immediate evidence of the wound that had killed her. I knelt to examine more closely. The fatal bullet had entered near her frontal lower neck. The point of entry was just under her chin about two inches wide near the collar of her cornflower blue blouse. The wound was a soft rose color.

I steadied myself as I knelt on the concrete brick doorway. I had never before seen a person who was murdered, let alone a young student in my charge. A counselor held out a chart indicating that her name was Christina Menefee, a tenth-grade student.

"A real sweetheart," my counselor said.

Propped high at right angles to Christina's head and about six feet away lay another student, Lydia Dew. She was still breathing, taking her last breaths before she succumbed.

All I could see were the gaping wounds and the sweet young faces of my own daughters who had attended high school, one of them at this very same school, a few short years ago. How could this violence solve any problem in the mind of a student?

Becky Rowan, the counselor, handed me another chart saying in a broken voice, "I was so, so worried about Luke, but I never! Would have never!"

Oscar took the chart from her and guided her to her counselor's office. She sank into a chair, put her head and arms down across the neatly stacked chart, and began to cry.

My first coherent thought was how often innocent people are made to suffer for someone else's irrational reasons.

Emergency personnel were bent over, working diligently to repair the damage made as the result of the gunshot wounds to Lydia Dew's torso and upper arm. Later we learned she was not an intended target but was somehow the second one shot after Christina. Christina had a few dates with Luke and was the main payback victim. Lydia and Christina were friends and had just happened to be together at the Commons at the moment of the attack.

Maybe in an urban inner city, I kept thinking while rustling through Luke's file. Maybe in some third world countries, a barefoot twelve-year-old with a sub-machine gun or a rocket launcher . . . but in the Bible Belt South? I was also struggling to control a tremor in my hand holding the chart, I wanted to yell, pound the chart into the concrete block walls. Not in Mississippi. Certainly the hard nature of the reality I saw was not happening in my school district.

As I looked toward the principal's office across the commons, suddenly I spotted my principal Roy Balentine. He was slumping in his office doorway near the reception room. Roy had been approved by the school board just three months ago, on July 1. This was his first assignment as principal, a big promotion from assistant principal at a much smaller school, Pearl Junior High, where he had served for three years. He was thirty-seven years old and needed my support and encouragement to battle all the critics one always faces in this position. Some expressed concern that he didn't have the experience for a big-time high school position. Would he adjust quickly enough to the demands and pressures of the job? I knew also I had responsibilities for his welfare because I had recommended him for the promotion. I kept the chart but moved toward his office entrance.

"Come on Roy," I said, "let's go in your office for a second."

"Where's Joel," I asked referring to our other assistant principal, Joel Myrick, whom I hadn't seen since arriving on campus.

Roy informed me that Joel had apprehended the shooter, Luke Woodham, who had been arrested.

Joel, I later learned, only loaded a single round in his service pistol. As I talked to Roy, Joel was at the police station downtown giving testimony along with a group of teachers who were on the scene at the time of the shooting.

Joel came out of his office near the front entrance and when he heard the shooting, he debated whether he should try to apprehend Luke immediately or wait until he left the building. Since Joel was a National Guard officer, he remembered that his service revolver was in his truck in the parking lot. While the shooting was in progress, he slipped past the action in the commons, ran to his truck, and picked up his .45-caliber pistol.

He quickly ran to the back entrance where he suspected Luke Woodham would exit the building. By the time Joel got to the back entrance Luke had exited the building and was attempting to drive away in his car. Joel ran to the front of Luke's car, pulled his weapon out and demanded that he stop. Joel made Luke get out of the car. He then placed him outside on the ground, putting his hands behind his back and waited until the police came to make the arrest.

I learned later that three of our students may have saved more lives. Michael Price, a senior who was in Algebra II, grabbed a teacher out of the line of fire. Jason Barton tried to tackle Luke Woodham while he reloaded. And as Woodham tried to flee, Justin Barnett, a junior, used his car to block his escape, which enabled Joel to apprehend him.

An hour and a half after the attack, a young Pearl detective, Aaron Hirschfield, obtained Luke's video taped confession. Luke was put on a suicide watch and his shoes and laces were removed. Barefoot, he wept as he told Hirschfield what he did.

"She's the first person I shot. Got her right in the heart," he said referring to Christina, who broke up with Luke a year before. In fact, he never shot her through the heart, but that was his intent.

The first phase of law enforcement's job was done. They had a confession from the shooter. Later they arrested students and a community college student as co-conspirators, which we'll look at in the next chapter.

My day, though, was just beginning.

The apprehension of Luke by Joel Myrick was a made-to-order hero story. He may have saved lives, but I knew I would soon be facing news reporters explaining why an administrator had a .45-caliber revolver on campus. We had our first news conference at 4 p.m. that day and it was the first question the media asked me. It was important for me to secure the facts as quickly as possible and reassure the community, and especially the parents, that their school would be safe again. It's not that I wasn't concerned about the direct effect on our students and their families, but I was the superintendent with responsibilities I had to fulfill that I would have rather set aside but couldn't.

The aftermath of the tragedy and the ensuing national media coverage found us ill prepared as our bad news quickly spread by radio, television and word of mouth. There's much to be said about this whole dimension of our experience, but this book is not about *reaction* but *preparing to prevent* an attack and intervening in a student's life before he or she ever plans a violent Random Actor attack.

———•———

The phone lines were jammed with every parent in the Pearl community trying to reach the school. Before meeting with the press, I did what I would have liked to have done for me had I been a parent. I requested a quiet office and having been shown it, went in and locked the door. I didn't want to speak to the secretary or anyone else—just to the parents. Then Becky, our counselor, gave me the parents' home and work numbers of the nine students who died or were wounded. I called and talked with each parent briefly as they were available, and invited them to come to the school immediately to meet with me. This took longer than I expected. I also reached out to our school attorney, Skip Jernigan, but parents came first, of course.

That task accomplished, I lowered my own head to my hands and prayed for wisdom in the decisions I would make that day and the ones I would make in the near future concerning the students, parents, and citizens of the Pearl community. I had been Pearl Public School's superintendent for 17 years; this community had been good to me and my wife of thirty-nine years, and my two daughters. I wanted to do all I could to take care of Pearl's citizens.

CHAPTER 6

THE KROTH GANG

———•———

O nly a few days after the attack, we were dealing with another frightening scenario: It was believed that a local youth gang plotted the attack and that more lives might be in jeopardy. In a small-town environment like ours, such a notion is unnerving. It's not as though there are a few dangerous individuals among hundreds of thousands—rather, it might the young fellow next door.

I found that one reason the gang connection is significant is that stopping Random Actor attacks is one issue, and stopping gangs and gang formation is another. And each may require different kinds of interventions.

Some Random Actor campus attacks have been the result of one student—for example, the attacks in Paducah, Kentucky, and Springfield, Oregon. Other attacks—Pearl, Columbine, and Jonesboro, Arkansas, for example—were the product of two or more youths committing a crime. In other words, they were the product of gangs—more specifically, Random Actor attack gangs.

In 1996, after the release of his book *Suburban Gangs—The Affluent Rebels*, Dan Korem wrote an op-ed piece that appeared in over a hundred newspapers across the country in which he concluded: "The choice is preemptive action now, or engaging in a new uncontrolled form of terrorism in the future—the very near future."

He pointed out that Random Actor gangs are not street gangs, like inner-city gangs that fight over turf, but they do meet the definition of a youth gang: two or more youths gathered together in a specific context and whose activities include, but are not limited to, criminal acts.[1]

As you will see, the interventions to stop Random Actor attacks and gang formation can overlap and one can help mitigate the threat of the other, but they are different. Thankfully, preemptive action can thwart both.

In this chapter, I will detail some of the general themes of Pearl's "Kroth" gang, as they liked to call themselves. (The material in this chapter regarding the Kroth gang was drawn from court records and testimony, statements to police, as well as from news accounts.)

Korem's research found that there are essentially three types of gangs in suburban and small-town communities:

Delinquent gangs: Engage in more generic types of crime like theft, drug selling, assaults, and other forms of violence.

Occultic gangs: Have attachments to beliefs in occultic powers.

Ideological gangs: Have attachments to a specific ideology, like a racist skinhead gang.

Columbine's Random Actors represented, essentially, a delinquent gang, while Pearl's Kroth gang combined delinquent and occultic gang elements.

———————◆———————

At first it was portrayed that Luke Woodham was a member of a cult-like group called Kroth, led by Grant Boyette, a local eighteen-year-old at Hinds Community College. *The Chicago Tribune* on October 9 published a story entitled: "Talk Turns to Devil Worship in Slayings, Death Plot at Mississippi School." This article wasn't much different from the articles in the home newspapers, except now our tragedy had leapt to the national front. The word was out that this was a satanic group and very few sources of substance existed on satanic cults but the little information that was present was no deterrent to the ever-hungry press.

As we saw, shortly after the Pearl murders, police arrested six of Luke's friends on October 7. They were all charged with murder-conspiracy. Brooks and Boyette were also charged with plotting the murder of Brooks's father.

Cults and drugs in Pearl were also cited in the local newspapers, but the group didn't fit any reliable definition of a cult. As the media peddled their articles, most police and school administrators denied there were cult and drug connections to Kroth.

The origin of the label "Kroth" elicited multiple theories. Some said that "Kroth" was derived from an Internet web site that also hosted the controversial role-playing game "Dungeons and Dragons." The site also hosted another role-playing game, "Dragon Spawn," set in a semi-medieval fantasy world. Kroth, which had the same general sound as earth, was the name of the game's imaginary world—where players created their own characters and used wondrous magic like an early medieval knight to challenge dragons or fight sword battles with strange creatures.

"Dragon Spawn" producer Jeffrey Naujok told the press that he had no affiliation with a satanic group, and he professed to be an ordained minister. He said he didn't condone violence and that the attack at Pearl High School was deplorable. Naujok said he had nothing to do with the slayings and that the media were seeking a scapegoat. He said he started creating "Dragon Spawn" in 1995 to be distributed free across the Internet.

Others claimed that the label Kroth was born in Grant Boyette's imagination, a local college student who surrounded himself with younger high school students, dictating his thoughts and philosophy to them. He was described as highly manipulative and persuasive in his control of younger boys.

Boyette's Sunday school teacher, however, said that "Grant was a quiet, polite, Christian boy." While he was at Pearl High School, Boyette would go into the cafeteria and, before eating, bow his head to pray. Many students took a cue from his actions, and the student-filled cafeteria would become quiet until Boyette's prayer was complete.

Beyond his façade of politeness and quiet demeanor, however—according to one of Boyette's friends—Boyette had an opposite, hidden, and private personality. He always wanted to play the game master, the friend said, but he didn't want to turn evil into good like most kids—he overturned the "happy ending." In the game he controlled, he made sure that evil won.

Grant's hero in history was Adolf Hitler, a "master" of influence for whom the end justified the means.

Grant had a temper and many of the former members of his group steered clear of him to avoid his wrath. Often he would say, "Don't make me do something I don't want to do," as he grabbed the offending person's neck and pretended to choke him.

Grant ruled that females were inferior and not to be trusted; so they weren't recruited as members. However, word had circulated among the members that Grant had turned to Satan after a broken relationship with a girl.

Nevertheless the group had no known satanic connections, no initiations, no rituals, no drinking of blood, no animal sacrifices, no sexual practices usually associated with the occult.

Grant's gang appeared to be motivated only by money and revenge. They needed money to accumulate resources for their goals of operation—namely communication, travel and personal satisfaction. They also developed an enemy list that would be the object of their violence.

Boyette told his followers the name Kroth didn't come from

his earthly father but from his real father, Satan. He described the occultic hierarchy as follows: first demons, then archangels, then generals, and then Satan. Boyette said he took his orders from Satan before passing them on to his gang. He used a five-pointed star inside a circle with three triangles inverted as their symbol. The big star in the middle was Boyette and the three triangles were the other members at the time.

Boyette dubbed himself the Master of High Demon Activity and said if he had a personalized car tag he would put MHD on it. If questioned, he would say it was short for "Mississippi Hound Dog."

In speaking to a possible gang recruit, he said, "If you are not with me, you are against me; if you are against me your are dead." Another reported paranoia-tinged remark was: "We can't move forward until all our enemies are gone." Christina Menefee, the first student Luke killed, was listed as Luke's "greatest enemy," according to a statement given to police by Donald Brooks the day after the attack.

Boyette set up a hierarchy of command with himself as the commander and Luke, Wes Brownell and Delbert Shaw as the top power members. Ranks changed depending upon circumstances and the actions needed.

Part of the code included a mandate that Kroth members keep discussion among themselves to a minimum, especially as related to the gang's plans. One of the members was severely reprimanded when he asked another member about group activities before discussing it with Boyette.

Besides those obvious control tactics, Boyette made special assignments to members of the group. Brooks said Boyette directed him to steal his father's credit cards and purchase a Nintendo 64, several laptop computers, scanners, car speakers, and radios worth an estimated $10,000. This is more in line with the delinquent gang type identified by Korem. (Similarly, Harris and Klebold were thieves who stole everything from bomb making materials to a computer, and who committed crimes of opportunity such as breaking into cars—in addition to illegally making explosives.)

The Brooks thefts proved to be a turning point for Boyette's Kroth. Only the credit card purchase for the Nintendo 64 game was completed. In order for the credit card companies to transact such large expenditures they called Don Brooks, Donald's father, to verify the order. He made Donald confess what was going on in his activities with Boyette and Luke. The Brooks family also decided Donald would immediately leave the Kroth gang, telling the members that he had turned to God and no longer wanted to be a member. In fact, Donald called his pastor, confessed that he had fallen from grace, and redirected his activities toward the church.

Donald said that Boyette's reaction to these developments was to set up a plot to kill Mr. Brooks, a charge that authorities later dropped.

Donnie and his father took their evidence to Pearl Police Department the first week of June 1997—four months before the shooting in October 1997. They also provided evidence of plans by the Kroth to shoot up the school.

After the attack, newspaper reports began to suggest the Police Department may have known—or should have known—about a possible shooting at the school prior to its occurrence in October. The Pearl Police denied any prior knowledge. After the trials of the co-conspirators and Luke Woodham's two trials, this point was never clarified. Brook's attorney continued making the accusations, and the Pearl police continued to deny.

The Pearl Police did admit, however, that information was discovered after the shooting that the Kroth, under Grant Boyette's leadership, had made plans since January 1997 to shoot up the school and avenge their enemies.

The original plan was to go into the school after the tardy bell had sounded and shoot their enemies. In setting up the plans, each group member had to find out where each "enemy" would be at the time of the attack. Boyette told the group they would launch the attack, and Donnie Brooks would drive the getaway car. The plans changed from time to time over the year as to which side of the school they would enter, the circled drive or the bus entrance.

Like Columbine killers Harris and Klebold, whose writings fantasized about flying a hijacked plane into the Empire State Building, these students had their fantasies. They discussed escape sites by truck to Mexico, by boat to Cuba, or just relocating in New Orleans. They would set up in the city, get odd jobs, and work until they were eighteen. Those were just some of their getaway schemes. Boyette said his grandparents would finance him, adding that they would give him anything he requested.

As mentioned, Luke Woodham's number-one enemy was Christina Menefee. He reported frequently to the group that she was continuing to bug him at school. The enemy list grew longer and continued to change.

A few of the Kroth members described Luke as possessed by spells placed on him by Boyette. When he disagreed upon occasion with Boyette's advice, Luke described himself as not being able to sleep, believing demons sent by Boyette had kept him up all night.

Nevertheless his friends speculated that Boyette was more attentive to Luke than the other members—probably because he was the easiest to control. Boyette himself testified that he held Luke and gave him companionship when no one else would.

During his trials, Luke claimed Boyette was under the influence of a satanic cult that exerted great powers over him. He also described himself as emotionally vulnerable, suffering from a troubled home life and a rebuffed romance when he first met Boyette.

Luke said Boyette told him, "I worship Satan, and Satan's

chosen you to be part of my group. You have the potential to do something great!"

He also testified that the acceptance of Boyette's influence and his group of friends transformed him from a student who failed his freshman year to someone who read books on astrophysics.

"I felt that I had complete control and power over a lot of things," he testified.

Luke's behavior patterns were substantiated during the trial: He had gained not only boldness and self-confidence in his actions, but also increased cruelty. Members of the group reported signs of increased cruel behavior before he murdered his mother and attacked the school. Luke's description of how he killed his dog, provided in Chapter 3, is one example of his heightened cruelty.

Desensitizing Luke to commit violent acts was alleged to be directed by Boyette. Luke said it started at his house before the killing of his dog. On one occasion Boyette held the dog allowing Luke to hit her repeatedly. On another occasion, Boyette held the dog in the air and instructed other members present to take their hits as the dog was passed around. It seems that the dog had a way of stopping at the feet of strangers, looking up at them, and turning one eye higher than the other. This action seemed to infuriate Luke and he would kick the dog or throw something at her.

This violent behavior continued in intensity and pace until Boyette and Luke finally killed the dog as detailed in Luke's "manifesto" documents.

In his testimony, Donald Brooks said that he believed Luke had to have had help with his final plan to commit the attack since he notoriously had trouble following directions and remembering rules at Dominoes where they had worked together.

This is only a partial account of paranoid and bizarre practices and manipulation in the Kroth, but it's a history that makes it difficult to know exactly what happened in the year leading up to the attack. That is common in these types of gangs, and the atmosphere is made even more volatile by the insertion into the group of one or more persons with the Random Actor profile.

Whatever led up to the attack, the courts ruled in the end. Here are the courts' decisions regarding the Kroth's six youths:

Luke Woodham pleaded innocent to all charges by reason of insanity. In the first of two trials, he was found guilty of the murder of his fifty-year-old mother and sentenced to life. In a second trial for the attack at Pearl High School, he was found guilty of two counts of murder and seven counts of aggravated assault. He received two life sentences and seven twenty-year sentences and will be eligible for parole when he is 65.

The murder-conspiracy charges against Justin Sledge, Wesley Brownell, Delbert Shaw, and Grant Boyette were dropped by Judge Robert Goza at the request of district Attorney John Kitchens, who said Mississippi's conspiracy law would be difficult to prove. Daniel Thompson's case was referred to the youth court because he was 16, and the adjudication of his case is sealed. All charges against Donald Brooks were dropped.

Boyette, the alleged ring leader, plead guilty to conspiracy to prevent a public officer for dischargning his official duties. He was sentenced to the Mississippi State Penitentiary at Parchman boot camp for six months and five years of supervised probation. Justin Sledge was sentenced to four months in a reform school.

None of the former Kroth who attended Pearl High School were allowed to re-enter. Each was provided private tutoring and took their final exams to finish their current school year.

Following the investigaton, three apparently left the area: Delbert Shaw, Wesley Brownell, and Daniel "Lucas" Thompson.

Grant Boyette dropped out of Hinds Community College but still resides in the Pearl-Brandon area.

Justin Sledge went on to attend Millsaps College as a religious studies major. In 2003, he was found guilty of possessing an unregistered machine gun and was sentenced to four months in federal prison, three months house arrest, and three years of probation. Earlier, Sledge had been charged with a misdemeanor, shooting his weapon from a public road.

The remaining Kroth member, Donald Brooks—whose family intervened in his Kroth gang membership—is now married, still active in a local church in Pearl, and (at the time this book went to press) expecting his first child.

Dan Korem says that in 1997, when the "affluent" gang trend in suburbs and small towns peaked, there were approximately 50–250 gang members for every 50,000 people in a community. His estimate is based upon data collected from police officers across North America, including: gang unit statistics, intelligence reports, and arrests. State-supplied statistics—from attorney generals and law enforcement agencies—have invariably been lower. Korem says the difference between his estimates and others is due to under-reporting.

"Many researchers in charge of these studies told me that they knew that local communities were severely under-reporting to protect their image," he says. "Today, the gang ratio is closer to 50–150 per 50,000, which is significantly lower than in 1997, but it has been rising steadily since about 2006, because there are now more teenage males of prime crime-committing age."

"Females," he adds, "account for only five to fifteen percent of gang members."

Thankfully, Pearl has always seemed to be on the low end of these statistics, but daily reports across North America confirm Dan's observation that the "affluent" gang trend is back on the rise.

To summarize: For communities to prevent Random actor attacks, two issues require attention. The first is the prevention of a Random Actor attack. The second is the prevention of gang recruitment and formation—which, as it did in Pearl and other communities, can provide the fertile ground upon which to grow both Random Actors and Random Actor attacks.

CHAPTER 7

VISITS TO LUKE

———•———

Even though it's in the Deep South, Mississippi can be cloudy and cold in January. In January 2007, it was cloudy and bone chilling when I went to the Mississippi State Penitentiary in Parchman, Mississippi, known as Parchman Farm. Parchman is the only location in the state where death row inmates are executed.

No doubt, some of my former students had probably found themselves inmates here. I know that some of my principals conducted field trips here with students as a lesson in the blunt realities of crime and criminals. In all my years, though, as a school superintendent I had never had a reason to visit the penitentiary. Now I had a reason. I wanted to hear from Luke Woodham, face to face, if there was anything we could have done to have prevented the attack.

Following a sleepless night, I thought about the conversation I was about to have with my former student. I would first establish the reason for the visit and then talk with him about the role bullying played. I wanted to ask Luke about life in prison and his safety and well being. Did he hear from his family and friends since his incarceration? Were there any teachers or administrators who positively influenced him during his school attendance? And most important, what had gone so wrong in his life that it resulted in the murder of three people and wounding seven others during his killing frenzy.

After I parked my car at the visitation center, I was instructed to leave all valuables behind in the car. I then handed over my car keys as you would have at a coat check and was given a numbered token. The visitor processing moved me from one stage to another until finally I was searched for weapons in a small room by an elderly guard. This was done near a sign which read "The Shakedown Area." The restroom signs read "Male" and "Female," as if there were no ladies or gentlemen in such a setting. The visitors like me who had scheduled visits then departed the Visitation Center in a shuttle van. We were dropped off about a half mile away at Units 29 and 32. Luke was in Unit 32.

As I waited to see Luke, I reflected on the harshness and starkness of such a place. This entire facility reminded me of a cattle yard or possible staging for the movie *Cool Hand Luke*. After about twenty minutes the inmates appeared on the opposite side of a solid wall partitioned by glass windows. There were white telephones in each of ten designated visitation areas. We were given about an hour for our visits. None of the visitors were allowed a pad or pencil inside the prison, so I will summarize what Luke told me.

Luke and I immediately recognized each other, but he wasn't the youngster I remembered from nearly ten years ago; he was now a fully-grown young man. He was six feet three inches tall and weighed two hundred and sixty pounds. He appeared neatly dressed in his solid white prison uniform, possessing a slight black beard and a well-groomed haircut with brilliant white teeth. I was surprised that Luke was handcuffed during our visit despite the wall separating us. The cuffs kept Luke from holding the phone, so he wedged it between his shoulder and ear. He was pleasant and courteous.

Due to nervousness and lack of sleep, I had to remind myself not to do all the talking. The purpose of the visit was to hear from Luke. Often people in positions of authority such as mine have not perfected the art of listening. My wife has reminded me, on occasion, that I fit this category. Now would be my chance to ask Luke the question that had persisted in my mind for nine and a half years. I had to listen carefully to his answer. I started our visit by discussing the tragic incident gently, especially the bullying.

Luke said that from day one at school he felt he was constantly harassed. He explained that the more he had tried to free himself, the deeper he got into trouble. If he tried to fight back or defend himself, he received the same punishment as those who had started the bullying. School was in no way fun or enjoyable for him, and he was miserable most of the time.

When I pressed him about the bullying, he broke down. It was my intention to get an assessment and not cause him an unpleasant flashback. Luke's reaction confirmed the conclusions I had drawn from years of research and analysis of bullying: the years do not erase the scars. So distressing was this subject for Luke that I didn't inquire further. I decided to wait for another visit.

I then asked him about his contacts since his confinement. Luke said his father had visited but his brother, now a truck driver living in Alabama, had not. Luke mentioned that none of his friends from his home area had visited or contacted him.

When I brought up the subject of his mother, Luke said his original intent was only to tie her up so he could take the family car to school on the morning of the incident. He said that Grant Boyette, however, told him to kill her, "so I did."

I asked Luke to identify the main cause of his crime. I expected him to cite his failed romance with Christina Menefee. Or perhaps it was his father's leaving the home after his parents' divorce. Instead, Luke stated that satanic worship had caused him to act as he did, a fascination that began in 1996, almost a year before the shootings. A specific event had convinced him of the reality and power of Satan.

Three boys had picked on him almost daily at various places, including his home. Since bullying was a longtime source of his discontent, Luke asked Boyette to help him solve his problem. In June, three months before the attack at Pearl, Boyette gave Luke a pentagram and instructed him to place one thumb on each side, hold the pentagram in the middle of his forehead, and pray to the devil for relief from his tormentors. The next day, one of Luke's bullies, Rocky Brewer died after being run over by a car (no connection to Boyette) while crossing the street in Flowood, a community near Pearl. Satan had answered his prayer. Luke's subsequent boldness derived from his newfound involvement in satanism.

I asked Luke if any changes had taken place in his thinking since the incident. He said he renounced his devil worship and that he was now a Christian.

As we ended our visitation, I asked him the one question that had haunted me for nearly a decade.

"As superintendent of schools, could I have done anything to prevent this tragedy?"

Luke looked at me and with clear eyes and no hesitation, and answered, "No, Doctor Dodson, not really."

As I rode in the van back to the prison Visitation Center my emotions ranged from anxiety to sympathy for this person who has ruined his life with the choices he made.

I thought about how Elvis Presley's father had been incarcerated here for three years on a charge of forgery. During the 1960s the freedom riders who attempted to end the desegregation of public facilities were arrested and jailed here for their Jim Crow crimes. And now, my student, Luke Woodham, was serving three life sentences for murder.

If I had thought the visit would bring me the relief of closure or the feeling of having been unburdened, I was wrong. There were only more questions. There would have to be more visits.

In January 2008, I received a letter from Luke:

Dear Dr. Dodson

Enclosed is a visitation approval form. As always, before you visit, call a few days ahead and make sure everything is alright. Well, I hope that you had a Merry Christmas! It was alright here. I got to relax a little bit and watch some football.

I heard from Christina's father. He wrote me telling me that he forgave me and was sorry for what he said about me on TV, I wrote him back and apologized to him anyway. I thought that you maybe might like to know about that.

I don't know if I told you or not but they started a school building here and I'm a tutor. They are also going to start having Bible College here. They have been doing it in Unit 30, which is a general population unit, and now they want to do it here. I'm supposed to be on the list for it. I hope that they let me in. The guy, who's doing it, Dr. Johnny Bley, had two spiritual growth classes in E building. I participated as a student in the first one and as a mentor in the second one. It's done by the New Orleans Baptist Theological Seminary and you can get a real degree from it. I guess that's about it from here. Write when you can.

Your Student,

Luke

My last visit to Luke was on February 26, 2008, about a year later. The units within the prison are arranged according to offense, and Unit 32 houses the most serious and violent criminals, those who require the highest level of security in the Mississippi prison system. Luke lives in Unit 32.

Since our last visit, the unit recorded one suicide and three murders resulting from attacks by inmates against other inmates.

A mop handle was fashioned into a spear, and was then used as a murder weapon. One inmate hanged himself by using bed clothing tied to the ceiling of his cell. In the summer of 2008, Unit 32 had become a battleground. I wanted to visit Luke sooner, but stayed away due to reports of violent conduct.

A few inmate protection organizations along with the ACLU brought a suit against the state for what they called inhumane treatment to prisoners. During my second visit, Luke told me of the methods used by the authorities to control the violent conduct of prisoners. When there were allegations of misconduct, the inmates lost privileges or freedoms. These losses might include fans during the hot weather, exercise time during breaks, television, reading materials, etc. Whenever restrictions came, the ACLU then claimed unjust and severely harsh treatment by authorities. Instead of improving, the situation got worse.

Nine visitors were bused to Unit 32. The procedure for visitors was about the same. We left all our possessions in our cars at the visitor parking lot, bringing with us only our keys, drivers' licenses, and our permit slips. The day before had been warm, and I didn't bring a coat with me, Today, I needed it. A heavy cool breeze was blowing through the prison compound. As I thought of my mild discomfort, I recalled that some of these prisoners would be here the rest of their lives with few comforts at all.

In the waiting area I listened to the talk of mothers and fathers here to see their sons. They openly talked to me about the years of imprisonment. One mother told about her son who had been imprisoned since he was eighteen and had twenty years more to serve. She spoke about having been overjoyed at the trial because the judge had given her son forty years instead of life imprisonment. This mother explained how a lockdown imprisonment with good behavior could reduce some of the time yet to serve. She had chosen to hire an attorney, borrowing on her house, to pay for the chance to help her son get out sooner.

Luke was given three life sentences without parole plus twenty years each for the seven students he injured on that October morning in 1997.

As before, there were ten partitions to fill, and the chatter coming from the ten conversations combined was so loud I could hardly hear Luke. I immediately noticed that he was not shackled and his hands were free to hold the phone. During my previous visit, both Luke's feet and hands were shackled. He explained that prison authorities had relaxed the rules to encourage better conduct from the inmates. There were clear signs of improvement. Luke seemed delighted by the opportunity to talk with more freedom and ease of movement. I, too, felt more relaxed and better prepared for my visit with Luke.

I had about twelve questions I wanted to ask Luke. Some were left over from the previous visit; others were new. Because I couldn't carry a pad or pencil inside the prison, I used an old school mnemonic trick, making up a word in which each letter represented the first word of the question I wished to ask.

I'm not an expert on interviewing, but the key is to lead the subject into doing the talking while the interviewer keeps the questions in order. Psychiatrists have told me to be aware of neurological or physiological disorders which are often present in prisoners who have served long years of confinement.

"Luke, I am trying to think of the best way to ask these questions, and I do not want to say anything wrong," I started out. "If I do, you certainly do not have to answer the question and please forgive me if there is any harshness in the question's content."

I told Luke I wanted to talk about the contents of his letter, especially the part about his religious experiences and his contact with Christina's father. I said I had a number of questions I wanted to ask and if he was in agreement, we would do the questions first. He indicated his approval to proceed in that manner.

"Can a person have priorities in prison?" I asked. "Can his life have purpose? Can he have hope?"

Luke said that priorities are limited because of the rules and regulations that restrict movement and access in his prison confinement. As for hope and purpose, he said they can be achieved when you are a disciple of Jesus Christ. No matter where you are, the spirit will be with you at all times.

After hearing his answers, I concluded that Luke was not the same person I had talked with a year ago. He was confident and upbeat, and his connection to his newly found religion was changing his life. Luke was like a young child enamored by his faith. I could sense his excitement while he answered my questions. Additionally, this opportunity to be exposed to religious doctrine was not Luke's alone. The prison officials had allowed the seminar instructors from a New Orleans church association to come in and conduct religious sessions for the first time in Unit 32. Perhaps there are concerns in using religion to control the inmates, but I could see that it was working—at least in Luke's case.

"You have a lot of thinking time and reading time in prison. What do you think about and what do you read?" I asked.

He said his thoughts were often on why he was in prison and how he got here. Some of those thoughts he couldn't act upon, but he did have control over himself and his own feelings. His reading time was limited by the scarcity of library facilities. He had little interest in novels but liked history and documentaries. He had recently attempted to read the Bible and the other religious books provided by the prison.

"What does your faith mean to you? How were you brought to know the Lord? Do you think Satan is real?"

His faith was the most important thing in his life, he conveyed. His relationship with God was a personal connection and was not controlled or changed by the thoughts and actions of others. Luke said he was brought to the Lord after he was arrested for crimes and placed in jail in Rankin County. His cellmates had asked the usual questions: what Luke had done and what he had been charged with. Without hesitation they began to witness to him. They asked him if he wanted to become a Christian believer. As with a lot of things that have happened to him, Luke believed some divine spiritual force was beginning to take control of his life. He had begun to read a Gideon Bible placed in the cell even before the cellmates began to talk with him.

Luke accepted the Lord after his witness encounter with those two cellmates. He now felt he was moving in the direction of denouncing his connection with satanic beliefs, although he remained convinced that Satan was real. He said that the absence of Christ is darkness and that without Christ, Satan will control our lives as happened in his own life before he accepted Christ.

"If you were giving someone pointers on how to identify a troubled student before he turns violent, what advice could you give me?" I asked.

He felt this was a difficult question to answer. In his case, all his stresses and emotions were interior. Violence was the release from this inner torment. If someone or some force could have calmed the feelings, help would have been possible. In Luke's case there was no relief from his misery and depressed feelings.

I asked Luke who believed in him when he was young and in what school subjects he had excelled.

His life had started out great, he said, with supportive parents and an enjoyment of school in the first few grades. Mrs. Mary Smith and Mrs. Pricilla Prather were elementary teachers who were encouraging. In junior high Mr. Marvin Oglesby was another encouraging influence. At the end of each grading period Mr. Oglesby invited all of his students to discuss report cards. He often talked to Luke and told him that with just a little more effort Luke could make straight As in his subjects. Luke liked history and mathematics best of all.

I asked Luke if he cared what people thought of him, what good could come from this tragedy, and whether he thought Grant Boyette should be serving in prison instead of him.

He said he cared what people thought about him, but had little control over anyone's thinking and no way to change it. As for the good that resulted from this, six students came to know the Lord after Lydia Dew's funeral, one of the two girls he murdered. Christina's father had become an ordained minister since his daughter's death.

Regarding Grant Boyette, Luke said he deserved prison for his role, but he had no control over those matters. Very little of his time had been spent thinking in that direction.

"Can you take me into what life was like in 'The Kroth'?" I asked. "Could you paint me a picture of what happened that day, how you saw things, how you felt, what you were thinking?"

Satanic worship he found interesting and fascinating at the time. He felt he was finally living the important life that made sense. Grant was their leader and they believed in him and his often-irrational thinking. Before the incident at Pearl High School, Luke remembered that Grant asked the group, "How many students do you think we could kill if we made that effort one day?" Luke said the murder of his former girlfriend was the only planned action; the others were hit by bullet fragments when he fired at random.

I wanted to pursue this line of questions, but they weren't easy for Luke to talk about, as was the case with the bullying questions at our first session. I sensed it was time to move away from the topic.

I did spend some time, though talking to Luke about Christina's father's who contacted him and forgave him for murdering his daughter.

Luke explained that Mr. Menefee's wife had died about a year after the incident at the high school, and that Mr. Menefee had moved to Florida and had become a minister. Luke, in turn, apologized to Mr. Menefee for what he did and thanked Mr. Menefee for his forgiveness. Mr. Menefee had apologized to Luke for the things he had said about Luke on television after the shooting.

The remainder of our conversation on this day concerned Luke's excitement about courses being offered at Unit 32 by the New Orleans church affiliated association. Inmates were now able to take courses in English grammar, books of the Bible, disciple making, and Christian doctrine.

At his tier church, Luke had given one of the Sunday messages about the Prophecies of Christ. Luke stated that he was not a preacher but considered himself a good teacher. He was excited about the new efforts made by his warden to bring more religious emphasis to his unit.

I told him to be careful for his own safety and to stay with his friends instead of conversing with a lot of strangers. Luke said that to be a disciple of Christ he had to reach out to others, and he wanted to do what a Christian should do.

If only Luke had undergone such a transformation before the mistake of October 1, he could now be on his way to a new life. Unfortunately, life does not work in that way, and Luke must pay dearly for his earlier mistakes. Before I left the meeting area, I prayed for Luke's safety and his continued involvement in being a disciple of Christ.

Some of our stories about youth are enjoyable to read and enjoyable to tell, and many demonstrate great success and reward for effort. This one, however, is different. This story is sad, and the sadness stems from the notion that it could perhaps have been prevented, could have turned out differently. Of course there is no way for it to be corrected. Possibly, Luke is trying in his own way to say something to the world. Perhaps Luke feels he has the ability through Christ to serve the one who saved him. Regarding his past, his life only amounted to death.

Once again I left Luke and Parchman and returned to my home and family. Will I visit Luke again? Right now, I don't have an answer.

What I do know, though, is that there is a solution that can stop school attacks and give parents confidence in knowing they will see their children after school. This is the subject of the next three chapters.

CHAPTER 8

THE RANDOM
ACTOR PROFILE

———•———

W
hat is it about bucolic, safe neighborhoods that really sets off the perpetrator of Random Actor violence? Until we can answer this question and how to identify the Random Actor profile, we will be unable to reach these students before they plot and commit violence. Once equipped with this knowledge, however, we can develop best practices, through training and evaluation of results, that can be used in any setting.

In the next three chapters, we'll listen to the researcher mentioned earlier, Dan Korem. What he has identified that stops school attacks isn't just a theory; it delivers results and has stood the test of time. I think what you'll learn is not only informative but also fascinating.

We also mentioned earlier that FedEx *doesn't* have mass shootings but the Post Office does—even though both are in the delivery business. Why is this? When Korem discovered the answers, he also discovered how to stop school massacres and threats through an easy-to-apply 3-point intervention. Today, educators and school administrators whimsically call this *doing the FedEx thing*.

It began in the early 1990s when human resource managers across the across the country asked Korem, a profiling expert, to solve the mass shooter riddle in the workplace. Places like Xerox had company massacres, and they didn't know how to prevent them. They tapped Korem for assistance because they were already using the *Korem Profiling System* for making hiring decisions to identify best-fit candidates.

Korem developed that system when members of the Young Presidents Organization asked him to engineer a system for negotiating contracts abroad—especially when the principals couldn't speak the local language. They wanted a rapid-fire system that enabled them to quickly profile people and identify in a few minutes of interaction how a person is likely to communicate, operate, and make decisions—without racial or ethnic stereotyping. Korem's system of four quick reads yielded a two-page profile that not only tells you how a person is likely to act, but also gives you quick suggestions how to interact, sell, confront, etc.

Korem's company, Korem & Associates, helped major organizations use his system for productivity applications: sales, negotiations, team leadership, and so on. As a former coach, I am especially intrigued by how professional, collegiate, and Olympic coaches use his system to improve athletic performance. Globally, more professionals have been trained to use his rapid-fire system than any other in the world—over 35,000.

Korem's system was published in his 1997 book, *The Art of Profiling—Reading People Right the First Time*, which also forecasted the Random Actor student-led attacks (an expanded, updated second edition was released in 2012). Four months later, the Pearl attack occurred. That same week he received his first calls for assistance from school administrators who had heard his predictions. Some of those who called had had frightening near misses. What was confusing was that the trend appeared as the juvenile crime rate was *dropping*.

Korem warned that student-led mass shootings/bombings *wouldn't* strike urban communities, but they *would* strike suburbs and small towns. He knew these communities well because of his research for his book, *Suburban Gangs*. (Ironically, one of the first suburban drive-by shootings occurred at his daughter's high school in Richardson, Texas, a Dallas suburb, on November 6, 1992, during which one student was murdered.) He also accurately predicted which schools wouldn't have attacks and threats *and why*. He even found an entire population of schools that were "doing the FedEx thing" that rarely had Random Actor massacre threats—discipline alternative education schools. These are schools for at-risk students in many school systems. This prediction caught everyone by surprise because that is where you would expect troubled students to act out.

"Believe it or not, the safest schools on the planet from a Columbine type massacre are the alternative discipline education schools that by definition only educate at-risk students," Korem explains. "This is remarkable when you think about it. If educators can prevent Random Actor attacks at the *highest risk* schools, then there's no reason they can't do it at *any* school. You simply have to know how to identify students with the Random Actor traits and provide the 3-point intervention."

Korem's research, which uncovered that most mass school shooters, suicide terrorists, and postal/company shooters have the Random Actor behavioral profile, is explained in detail in his book *Rage of the Random Actor* (2005). This chapter and the next two condense his research on school attacks from three chapters in that book, and this chapter is provided in a Q-and-A format. Specific terms are capitalized for clarity; they are not adjectives, but are terms from the *Korem Profiling System*.

I am certain that if our counselor, Becky Rowan, and Luke's teachers had known this profile and the intervention, Luke would have received assistance, he would have responded, and young lives would have been saved. I'll always be haunted by what Becky said as she stood over Christina and Lydia: *I was so, so worried about Luke, but I never! Would have never!*

PERFECT STORM BREWS IN NORTH AMERICA AND EUROPE

Two months before Columbine, you warned principals at the February 1999 National Association of Secondary School Principals conference that Denver suburbs were one of the highest risk targets in North America for an attack with explosives. You even said it could be on the scale of the 1995 Oklahoma City bombing. How did you make that prediction?

I spent some time in those suburbs in the 1980s and early 1990s for my book, *Suburban Gangs*. At the conference, I showed a video clip of suburban Denver teens who committed a Random Actor attack in 1997, murdering a police officer and civilian picked out at random. It was the only video clip I showed as an example of where a major attack might occur. Not because Denver suburbs were a determinate target, but a likely high risk target. I also spent time in a clinic for high risk kids in one of the suburbs.

Then all through 1998, law enforcement officers across Colorado whom I had either trained or who knew of my research reported to me unrelated cases where kids with the Random Actor profile were found with explosives and the intent to blow up their schools. I even received a call for assistance from the investigator's office at the Jefferson County District Attorney's Office where Columbine is located.[1]

Because of these reports I contacted the lead school safety official in Colorado and told her of the threats in February of 1999. She agreed that two-day workshops "on both sides of the mountains" be deployed to prevent an attack. After Columbine, she never returned phone calls and assistance to this day has never been provided in the state of Colorado.

Until the attack at Pearl, school attacks were rare and weren't a trend. Today, how many school threats are there a day?

Around the time of the Columbine Massacre, there were about 50 of these threats a day (which doesn't include prank threats). As the number of students with the Random Actor profile continued to increase, so did the number of threats. By the time of the "Batman Movie Massacre" in Aurora, Colorado, in the summer of 2012, it was about 100 times a day. Right after that attack, I called the executive director of the Texas Association of School Administrators, Dr. Johnny Veselka, who I regularly worked with since 1997 to help school districts successfully prevent attacks. I warned that the 2012–2013 school year would

In 2002, in the Dallas suburb of Plano, Texas, a student with a cache of explosives blew up this police car. He was caught by a professional trained to apply Random Actor violence prevention strategies before he could complete a school attack.

probably be the worst school year on record for threats and attacks. In the fall, threats escalated to about 150 a day—a 50 percent increase.

After the Newtown Massacre, they increased to over 250 a day, unprecedented in U.S. history, and they persisted through the spring of 2013, as did Random Actor slayings in the general population. On January 10, right after schools reconvened, the first school attack of 2013 hit Taft, California, a small town, and other school attacks soon followed.

As the trend has spiraled upward, there can be just as many prank threats a day and the line is blurring between pranks and threats that *are* made *with* malice where there may or may not be a planned attack.

This data is based upon surveys I conduct of educators and law enforcement professionals in various trend indicator locales. Only 10 to 20 percent of the non-prank threats find their way into media or state reportage.

For example, if you have twenty school superintendents in a room who know each other, there are usually one or two who have had a threat and their colleagues don't know about it. Part of the reason is that threats that occur in small towns that often don't have local newspapers. Others aren't reported for a whole host of other reasons such as a fear of setting off a panic or inspiring others, or concern about public perception that schools aren't safe, and so on. What is alarming is that the current number of threats (Spring 2013) is about *five times* greater than it was right before the Columbine massacre. This is in addition to hundreds of prank threats on a given day. This massive number of threats tells us that attacks will increase in frequency and in lethality unless we act to prevent them. The reason this should be viewed as a North American trend is that Canada also regularly has threats and attacks in its country of over 36 million. In Europe the trend has also steadily increased, followed by a number of massacres since 2002 in statistically safe countries like Finland and Germany. Tiny Finland, for example, with a population of only 5.4 million, has had several massacres.

How many school evacuations result from these threats and at what cost?

In Texas, for example, the second largest state with a population of 24 million and two-thirds the size of Canada, there are over 4 million students. From August through December 2008 there were approximately 100 to 150 school-year evacuations. By 2013, the rate was about double that. This was data gathered from intelligence sources in schools, law enforcement, and other safety-related specialists. The number of evacuations per capita is pretty consistent across North America. From a risk assessment perspective, even if half of the closings were just over-reactions, it is still an intolerable number. A major contributing factor to over-reaction is a lack of basic knowledge about Random Actor threats and how to investigate. Regarding the loss to the taxpayer, it's in the millions in Texas. The average cost to evacuate a 1,000-student high school can range from $10,000–$25,000 by the time you factor staff and facility cost, law enforcement response, and so on. Most states are experiencing the same number of evacuations per capita, and the cost of evacuations is more than what it would cost to initiate prevention training that stops student threats.

Since 1994, you've warned that you are more concerned about the use of explosives than guns. Why is that?

At-risk kids usually act with greater intensity than their predecessors when a trend continues over time. Today, you can build explosives with materials that are found inside a school using plans downloaded from the Internet. Metal detectors and the like won't help. People forget that Columbine was supposed to be a bombing incident. Harris and Klebold smuggled in two propane tanks with detonators. Had they worked, 400–500 students and staff would have died. You regularly hear of school districts and law enforcement agencies doing "active shooter" training. This training is useless to prevent a bombing attack, which is the greater long-term threat.

Why is Texas one of the last major states that hasn't had a massacre since 1997 when the trend started?

From 1997–2002, I targeted approximately 80 of the highest risk suburban and small town districts in Texas and provided Random Actor violence prevention training. This was facilitated at the urging of state education leaders like Dr. Johnny Veselka as well as suburban and small-town superintendents. In almost every case, threats stopped immediately. Some of these cases are cited in *Rage of the Random Actor*. For example, Nederland Independent School District with 5,000 students near Beaumont, had authentic threats (not hoaxes or pranks) after the Columbine massacre, as did thousands of other schools across North America. Once their staff was trained and they applied the intervention strategies, their threats stopped.

So why are the threats severely escalating in Texas and other districts across North America that used your strategies?

Staff attrition is the most common reason that sustained protection stops. It accounts for almost 90 percent of the failure to sustain protection in the school systems we trained. Most believe people inaccurately believe, however, that other issues, like a lack of funding, are the culprit.

On the 10th anniversary of the Columbine attack, I surveyed more than 200 educators, school administrators, law enforcement officials and corporate executives from across the country. When asked to select the most common reason for the resumption of threats and building evacuation *after* school districts/systems apply Random Actor violence prevention interventions, only 16 percent answered correctly, as shown by their responses:

1. Outrage by parents that interventions are being applied and request that interventions stop — 15%
2. Teachers inaccurately identify students as being Random Actor campus attackers and administrators stop interventions — 28%
3. Lack of Funding — 18%
4. Staff Indifference — 33%
5. Staff Attrition rate — 16%

Staff attrition rates in school systems range from about 8–15 percent. So it is common sense that when half or more of your staff doesn't know how to identify the Random Actor traits and apply the interventions that threats will return. And they did—across the country, not just Texas. School systems we trained across North America saw their threats return. It was like flipping on a switch.

Nationally, school superintendents turn over about every two to four years. So there isn't leadership to sustain and recharge the behavioral fire extinguisher. It's human nature that once all is calm and threats have stopped to put these things out of mind. I warned officials that unless they put in place a continuity plan for sustaining protection, their threats would return. And that's what happened. The only school district in Texas that didn't see its threats return was where the superintendent didn't turn over and he made sure his staff applied the strategies. We trained his district in 2000 and he hasn't had an evacuation in nine years.

In 2006, Nederland Assistant Superintendent Mike Guidry called when their evacuations resumed. So we trained his staff and again threats stopped because they knew what to do. They were intervening before a student ever fantasized about blowing himself up or committing a massacre with guns and bombs. I warned that this must be recharged every couple of years. Mike retired, the application wasn't sustained, and they just had an evacuation at the end of the 2009 school year. It's a predictable outcome.

You say that the safest locales, suburbs and small towns, are actually highest at risk for a Random Actor attack. Were those the districts you targeted from 1997–2002?

Yes. We didn't focus on urban communities, and the data proved accurate. And by small town, we mean towns as large at 50,000 or others that were larger but had a small town feel, like Tucson.

Only one urban community in Cleveland in 1997 had a Random Actor attack, but it was at the upscale magnet school for exceptional students. Later, I'll explain why almost every school massacre in North America and Europe since 1997 has occurred in suburbs and small towns.

Your strategies have also been successful on a large scale. Only one region in the United States didn't have school threats after

9/11, while thousands of schools did. What happened there and why do you think it was so successful?

It was a region in which more than 2,500 educators were provided Random Actor violence prevention strategies. The region, in northeast Texas, had about 50,000 students and experienced several serious close calls. What is significant is that many similar school systems surrounding that region that didn't apply the strategies did have threats like the rest of North America.

The reason for its extreme success was because *all* students with the Random Actor traits received intervention, not just those who made threats or were acting out (as explained in Chapter 9). I currently know of one school system that responds in a coordinated effort only if there is a threat to life and limb. While admirable, many of the students who make threats and are escalating aren't on a counselor's or police officer's radar. So it's not surprising that this big-city school system responds to dozens of threats a day because they don't get ahead of the curve to reach students before they ever fantasize or hatch a plot.

THE RANDOM ACTOR TRAITS

What are the Random Actor behavioral traits?

If I asked you to "profile" Queen Elizabeth II and identify whether she seems to prefer to control or express her emotions, the obvious answer is "control." She's easy to read because her trait is extreme. Well, it's the same with Random Actors who kill. They have two traits that are extreme and typically easy to identify. In virtually every case, you will find a behavioral paper trails months in advance of an attack.

If you'll follow along, I'll let you identify the traits.

The *Korem Profiling System* was originally conceived as an on-the-spot system that corporate executives could use for foreign negotiations. You make two quick reads and you identify how a person communicates—*his talk*. You make two more reads and you identify how a person prefers to operate and make decisions—*his walk*. So, which part of the Random Actor's profile will kill you? Which part of the profile should you focus on? His "talk"—how he communicates? Or his "walk"—how he operates and makes decisions?

That's pretty easy. His walk.

Correct. He kills with actions and decisions. Most news accounts immediately after an attack, though, focus on communication actions like *he was very polite* or *he seemed like such a nice guy*. But these observations don't tell us how he will perform . . . how he will act. So we don't look at how he communicates—that he's friendly, polite, well-mannered, etc. The content of what he says may be important, but how he presents himself may or may not be important.

Now let's identify the first of the two Random Actor "walk" traits. The first "walk" or performance trait can be found by answering this question: Does a person prefer to operate in a predictable/conventional manner . . . or . . . in an unpredictable/unconventional manner?

Most school attacks are homicidal-suicidal acts. So, is committing this type of attack a conventional or unconventional act compared to just getting in a fight?

A homicidal-suicidal massacre is an extremely unconventional act.

Correct again. Random Actors are extremely unconventional, like Luke Woodham, who was fixated on self-styled satanic rituals, or the Columbine killers, who displayed extreme creativity in how they plotted their attack. You'll often hear many descriptions of the unconventional trait: he is a bit odd or quirky; he is very creative; he's a free-spirit. In our rapid-fire system, we call this the Unconventional trait. This doesn't mean that it's easier or harder to "predict" what he or she is going to do, rather this person prefers to do things that are more outside-the-box and unconventional. That a person has this trait by itself isn't troublesome. It's when he or she has the dark side of this trait, like anarchism and recklessness . . . and it is combined with the second trait.

What is the second Random Actor trait?

The question we ask to determine the second trait is: Does a person makes decisions out of confidence or fear? We're not looking at how someone makes decisions in an area of competence, like academics or athletics. We want to know how he makes everyday decisions *separate* from his area of competence.

Steven Kazmierczak

When Luke complained about being bullied or the Columbine killers complained about being at the "bottom of the food chain," lashing out at anyone who was different from them, were they making decisions out of confidence or fear?

I'd say extreme fear.

Correct. In fact, virtually all school killers who commit mass attacks operate out of paranoia, what we call the high end of the Fearful trait. As noted by mental health professionals, the paranoia might be a diagnosable DSM IV condition like paranoid schizophrenia, or a person might be just plain fearful. Presently, most students who threaten or do commit attacks do not have a diagnosable condition, however. Some do, but most don't.

To summarize, students who commit attacks are extremely Unconventional and extremely Fearful when making decisions separate from their area of competency. Student Random Actors who kill always display the two Random Actor traits to the extreme, and there is always a visible behavioral paper trail before they attack.

Now if you could only change one of the two traits to avert an attack, which would you choose—the Unconventional or high Fearful trait?

I would want to address the student's paranoia as it seems that is what would cause the most agitation.

That's right. When educators as a group are asked this question, they get it right immediately because it's common sense. When we look at the 3-point intervention we'll see how important it is to focus on this trait.

Kazmierczak's tattoo

How difficult is it to identify someone with Random Actor traits?

Since 1997, we've never had a call from an educator who *mistakenly* thought a student had the Random Actor traits. This is because they are observing extreme actions. Here's a typical example that fooled a twenty-year veteran campus police chief, a leading criminal justice scholar, and the *Associated Press*; none could profile or knew the Random Actor traits.

On Valentine's Day, 2008, Steven Kazmierczak attacked more than 150 students in a lecture hall at Northern Illinois University in the sedate community of DeKalb, Illinois. He killed six (which included himself) and wounded eighteen others. He murdered with a shotgun he carried in a guitar case and pistols and ammunition strapped to his body.

The *Associated Press* led with the copy: "If there is such a thing as a profile of a mass murderer, Steven Kazmierczak didn't fit it: outstanding student, engaging, polite, and industrious, with what looked like a bright future in the criminal justice field." The reporter, like most, focused on Kazmierczak's communication actions and his area of competence. The campus police chief described him as a "fairly normal" person.

One of his former professors, Jim Thomas, a nationally recognized criminal justice scholar, said he met Kazmierczak in an introductory sociology class. He said: "In this large class he stood out. So I tried to use him as an unpaid assistant. He stood out because he was hard working, he was bright, and he would come up and *talk* about ideas behind what I'd taught."

Notice that this criminal justice scholar did the same thing most of us do: he looked at how Kazmierczak communicated and how he performed in his areas of competence. But, this is the wrong part of the equation. For years before the attack, Kazmierczak displayed the Random Actor traits.

He regularly displayed the high Fearful trait, going back to his high school days when he mutilated himself and was treated at a psychiatric center. He wore a large tattoo that displayed self-mutilation, which revealed both his high Unconventional and Fearful trait.

In college, he wrote a paper entitled: "Self-Injury in Correctional Settings: 'Pathology' of Prisons or Prisoners?" It examined why inmates self-injure themselves—cutters, for example.

If you tried to make a read on him by just his smile, how he talked to you, or his interest in his studies, you might never know how troubled he was.

But if you look at his tattoo and his paper, it would have been appropriate to inquisitively ask: This is an interesting topic. How did you come up with the idea? If a professor saw that he had the two traits, high Fearful and Unconventional, it would then be appropriate to find a way to provide help.

This easily applies to Luke Woodham and Eric Harris and Dylan Klebold at Columbine.

Overall, there was nothing about any of the three that is different from other school attackers who had the Random Actor traits.

Luke was obsessed with satanism and arcane literature—the Unconventional trait. It was also common knowledge that he had been bullied and isolated by his peers for years—the high Fearful trait. One of his classmates, Trey Bynum, said: "I remember when he started kindergarten, he got picked on every day. When we got to junior high, he still got picked on. They called him fat, chunky, and they used to jump him [start fights] all the time. When we got to the ninth grade, everybody still picked on him, and I guess he just finally blew up. He just got fed up with it all and snapped." The two Columbine killers notably demonstrated both traits. For example, Eric Harris faked his suicide to frighten a girl and regularly fantasized about ending the world. The teens created websites, suffered from depression, and Dylan created the moniker VoDKa memorializing his heavy drinking to numb his depression. They even irrationally ranted against the extremely confident Tiger Woods. In the 1990s, I used to ask students with the Random Actor traits who they liked better, Michael Jordan or Dennis Rodman, who regularly displayed paranoia. They always picked the dark and reckless Rodman. I'm certain the Columbine killers would have done the same. The book *Columbine* by Dave Cullen provides other examples.

I did report on one case in the Chicago suburb in *Rage of the Random Actor* where a student with the Random Actor traits recruited a student who didn't have the profile, but this is extremely rare.

Are all students with the Random Actor traits potential killers?

No. The best illustration I can give you was explained to me by Constable Dennis Reimer of Taber, Alberta, Canada. Eight days after Columbine, a fourteen-year-old boy at W.R. Myers High School, where Reimer was the student resource officer, killed a student and wounded another with a rifle. The boy complained about being bullied; he was new to the farming community of about 7,000. His mother was divorced and recently remarried. (Canada prohibits the publishing of a juvenile's name associated with a crime.)

I debriefed Reimer on camera and he said that he had no idea that the student was that troubled. He said he knew the boy was rightfully angry about the bullying. Reimer could grasp the fact that the lad had the high Fearful trait, but not the Unconventional trait. I kept pressing him to remember anything he did that was really unconventional, but all he could remember is that the lad didn't have much interest in anything and didn't dress oddly.

One last time, I pressed: *Can you ever remember a time when he did something really different?*

Reimer then recalled a day when the student came to school with his head shaved. When asked why he did it, he said, *I wanted the boys to like me.* It's well known in the field of psychology that under pressure we typically go to our actual traits because it's where we feel comfortable. In this case, he did something extremely unconventional. Later, it was discovered that he had a satanic website—another example of the high Unconventional trait.

When I asked Reimer if he thought all kids with the Random Actor traits could be dangerous, he said no. He then related the following "gun, bullets, and trigger" analogy that he uses with parents.

Some people have the behavioral profile of a hammer, which can be used constructively or destructively. Other people, however, have the profile of a cocked gun, the Random Actor profile, which by its very nature is potentially destructive. There's nothing constructive about a cocked gun.

But the gun can't fire without bullets. The bullets are the stressors in a youth's life: trouble at home, bullying, isolation, and so on. We work with these kids and we are pulling bullets out of the chamber by being there for them, listening, and interventions.

Once the chamber is filled, though, all you need is a trigger. Now most people and news accounts focus on the trigger: what made them go off. The reality, though, is anything can make them go off, which is why there is rarely a motive in the classic law enforcement use of the term.

Thankfully, most students with the Random Actor traits don't reach the point where the chamber is full, where they have explosives or guns and plots to kill. But virtually all the Random Actor school killers had all the ingredients because no one knew how to read the obvious . . . their Random Actor traits . . . and the 3-point intervention that takes away their rage and guides them out of the harmful profile.

What is it about these two wires—the two traits—that makes them spark, as you put it in your book?

By themselves, the two traits, high Fearful and Unconventional, aren't inherently combustible, although paranoia when making decisions is troubling for anyone. But, when the traits are combined, there is always a severe internal tension in the background.

Imagine that you like to be unconventional. You like to be different, distinguished from the crowd. But you are chained to indecision by your Fearful trait, which sets off all kinds of contradictory behavior. Separate from your natural skills and talents, you can't escape your deepest fears when you make decisions—unless you are in total control. You want to *do* something, but your decision-making is always saying, "not so fast . . . you know they're against you . . . you know they want you to fail." You feel cursed. Those who are not violent find themselves immobilized because they are afraid to commit—to a new career, a personal relationship, to anything where they don't have control. Others retreat where no one is an eyewitness to their insecurities, falling prey to groups that promise relief and safety from their own insecurities—from faddish groups to cults, often the freakier the better—because that satisfies their unconventional trait. Those who have an adept or pleasing communication side to their personality use it to mask their turmoil. As long as they operate in their area of competence, they are OK. But when they don't, that's when they become threatened and when their destructive behavior surfaces.

Why is the trend here and how many students have the Random Actor traits?

There are a statistically significant number of students with the Random Actor traits, about 2 to 4 percent of students in grades six to twelve. School counselors and mental health practitioners believe it is about the same percentage or slightly less in elementary school.

Until recently, I would have said 1 to 2 percent. This was based upon direct feedback from counselors and mental healthcare professionals we've trained. Most said they thought it was higher, but we stuck with this estimate. Now we know for a fact it is much higher.

The United States Preventive Services Task Force 2009 report concluded that two million teenagers are clinically depressed— about 6 percent of all students. When we look at the Random Actor traits, you'll see why the intuition of the counselors and mental health professionals was correct. This means that if you have 1,000 students in a high school, 2 to 4 percent or 20 to 40 students will have the Random Actor traits. Obviously, this doesn't mean they will all harm others, but it's the sheer number that keeps administrators up at night.

For about 90 percent of students with the Random Actor traits, family deterioration is where the high Fearful trait is cultivated. The typical risk factors include: divorce, separation, physical abuse, sexual abuse, one or more of the parents is severely dysfunctional, parents never married, and so on. Latch key homes are another factor

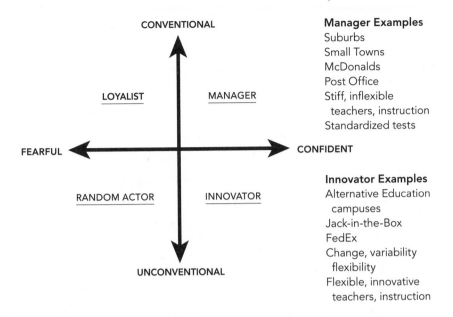

where a parent isn't at home after school, which is when most juvenile crime occurs (3–6 p.m.). And then you have homes where parents just aren't paying attention. While there is a very small percentage of students who are bent on evil, this is the smallest percentage.

Why do student Random Actors target suburbs and small town schools? Is there a pattern of who/what they like and don't like?

When you take the Fearful-Confident and Conventional-Unconventional gauges and put one top of the other, you get four quadrants that represent *performance* types—how people like to operate. Using common sense, which one of the other three quadrants will the Random Actor inherently dislike or hate and why?

The answer is the Manager quadrant. Why? Because it represents the behavioral opposite of the Random Actor. They have nothing in common. One is Conventional, the other is Unconventional. One is Confident, the other is high Fearful. In fact, many times people with the Random Actor traits can't clearly articulate why they target places, organizations, and people that represent the Manager quadrant. It's one reason why there rarely seems a rational motive for their crimes. Places or people that represent extreme confidence and predictability can just set them off. Here are examples:

- Suburbs—neatly cut lawns; people confident that they are safe and have money in their pocket; sedate shopping malls; safe neighborhoods
- Small towns—no change or variability; people are confident and secure and don't lock their doors
- Schools— same bells, same classes, same administration that is predictably in control without change
- Church—predictable Ten Commandments; confident faith in God

These equations tell us why there are shooters at the U.S. Post Office but not FedEx, or McDonalds but not Jack-in-the-Box which is out-of-the-box. The Post Office, like suburbs and small towns, represents the Manager quadrant. Anything that represents extreme Predictability and Confidence can set them off. In a company, for example, we see attacks in accounting departments and on assembly lines, but never in art departments. This is because the art department represents the Innovator quadrant and is not the behavioral *opposite* of the Random Actor traits—it shares the Unconventional trait.

As already noted, there has only been one urban mass shooting and it was at the upscale magnet school. In urban areas there is a lot more chaos and unpredictability. It's not settled. There are other factors, but here it's the Manager factor that is dominant.

Before the Virginia Tech attack, education and law enforcement executives from across Virginia identified Virginia Tech as their highest risk target using your grid. What happened?

In December of 2006, the police chief at William and Mary College said he had read my book and asked if I would present a workshop on how to prevent Random Actor attacks in January 2007. The audience was education and law enforcement professionals and executives from across the state. I was skeptical that he could secure attendance on such short notice, but the class was filled as he predicted, with about 50 professionals.

It wasn't my first experience in Virginia. In 2002, I had trained the senior staff at the University of Virginia where they had fourteen serious bomb threats. The presentation of the traditional campus built by Jefferson clearly represented the Manager quadrant. After the training, the senior campus executives said their threats stopped. At William and Mary, I hoped we could help the state get ahead of the curve.

After the first day of training, I asked the participants to look at the grid and identify the highest risk target in their state that represents the Manager quadrant. Immediately, they said, "Virginia Tech." The Manager attributes they identified included: state university, traditional, high number of technical disciplines, military presence on campus, and located in a small town. No one from Virginia Tech was present.

The chief asked if I would return and do another workshop in May. The Virginia Tech attack struck in April. One of the most tenured clinical psychologists from the university was present at the second training. He told me that he wrote an evaluation recommending that these strategies be deployed. His report was never read by officials. He left the university about a year later.

It's common in many communities after an attack to quickly try to move on rather than to deploy strategies to prevent another attack. In January of 2009, another Random Actor attack hit the campus. An economics student at Tech *beheaded* another student in the student café.

While the April attack that claimed 32 lives was underway, the police chief at one of Virginia's leading universities had the following conversation with his president.

President: What do you think about this?

Chief: The shooter is going to commit suicide, is affluent, and he has displayed very specific Random Actor behaviors that have been observed by others.

President: How do you know this?

Chief: I have been trained how to identify Random Actors and how to prevent and respond to Random Actor incidents.

When the chief asked to deploy the strategies across the campus, he was also turned down.

It was a community college student from Pearl who recruited Luke and the others into his makeshift gang. Should higher education campuses be working with K–12 campuses to prevent attacks?

Yes. When you have a college student who is a Random Actor operating out of fear, it's not uncommon for him to want to reach out and control those who are younger and easy to manipulate. This is what happened in Pearl where a community college student recruited teenagers, and I expect this trend to increase in the future.

How did you choose the identifier "Random Actor?" Were you thinking about the phrase "random acts of violence?"

Remember, the original application for our rapid-fire system was for negotiations abroad. The identifier was actually selected to give a CEO a clear picture of who *not to negotiate with*. The person will probably be unreliable and unstable because of the high Fearful trait and would innovate whatever was necessary to create the impression of confidence and stability.

By happenstance, it turned out that when I was asked to solve the company shooter equation, most had the Random Actor profile. So the identifier stuck.

Related to attacks by Random Actors, they may or may not target people they want to kill. They may frame their rage against those

Jonesboro attackers.

who represent the Manager quadrant, but once they start to kill, they may kill anything that moves.

I find it fascinating that students have also been freed where professionals have used your research and training.

That's right. Shortly after the 9/11 terrorist attacks, in Flowood, Mississippi, right near Pearl, a fourteen-year-old student was falsely accused by students of being a mass attacker. He was incarcerated as an overreaction by school officials and local police. A police officer we trained with the Fort Worth Police Department was the young man's uncle. He profiled his nephew and told me that his nephew didn't have the Random Actor profile and there was no evidence. He asked if I could assist, and the charges were eventually dropped.

In another national case in the Dallas suburb of Garland, an administrator overreacted to a student's allegation that a fifteen-year-old student was a bomber the day after Columbine. The student was suspended. The student's father asked me to intervene. I spoke to the superintendent, Jill Shugart, and within days he was reinstated and the potential of a huge lawsuit disappeared. Legal professionals explain that schools actually have less exposure than more exposure by applying this research. First, it prevents attacks. Second, the likelihood of false positives and stereotyping severely diminishes.

Do girls commit these attacks or make threats?

Thankfully teenage girls haven't committed an attack, but thousands have been arrested or suspended for making Columbine type threats. But this could change. We identified the techniques used by suicide terrorist cells to recruit women to commit a Random Actor attack, and this could become a trend in schools. One of the main reasons that we haven't seen female attacks is that they are statistically far less prone to commit acts of violence.

How young should we pay attention?

Elementary School. First, because teachers can reach out to these students with the 3-point intervention and apply it. Statistically, elementary school teachers have a much higher intuitive profiling accuracy than secondary school teachers because they focus more on development and understanding students, and they are terrific when applying intervention. And second, one of the first attacks was committed by Andrew Goldman, 11, and his classmate Mitchell Johnson, 13, at Jonesboro, Arkansas, in 1998. They set off a fire alarm, and as students and teachers exited the school, they fired on them from about one hundred yards away with scoped rifles.

Most people aren't aware that there were thousands of threats directed at schools by students after 9/11 and the Columbine attacks. Why did this happen?

This was due to what I call the Psych Ward Effect. It's a unique type of contagion of fear that sets off the paranoia of people with the Random Actor traits. These threats were inaccurately characterized as "copycat" by the media, suggesting that one person was copying another's actions. Less than 5 percent were copycat acts in which someone was copying another attackers actions. Here's what actually happened.

Imagine that a psychiatric ward has thirty stabilized patients, and you put a destabilized patient on the ward. What happens? They can all be set off, and they aren't copying one another. This is what happened in the schools.

Districts that applied the prevention strategies, though, didn't experience the Psych Ward Effect because their students were stable. If you try to stop these threats assuming that students are copying one another, in most instances you will fail. If you address these threats by reducing the paranoia of students with the Random Actor traits, you will succeed. That's why the region in Texas that applied the prevention strategies didn't have threats, but schools surrounding that region and the rest of the country did.

Why is recognizing the Psych Ward Effect important?

After the 2013 Newtown Massacre at Sandy Hook Elementary, thousands of threats followed as well as numerous multiple slayings. The trend hasn't changed since Columbine and 9/11. If schools don't reach their students *preemptively*, they can count on massive numbers of severely disruptive evacuations as well as follow-on attacks. Additionally, I've had to assist school systems that overreacted and threatened or incarcerated innocent students because of the intense climate of fear.

Why did you stop providing assistance and are now providing assistance once again?

I view this work as almost pro bono. When the second Intifada hit in Israel followed by the war in Iraq, I gave the time designated for education to our military. The reason I agreed to help in schools and higher education again is because of the severe number of threats. It's also likely that domestic extremists will recruit some of these students to commit attacks, similar to the "DC Sniper" duo in which a former vet recruited a teenager and terrorized an entire region of the northeast in 2002.

CHAPTER 9

THE 3-POINT
INTERVENTION

STOPS ATTACKS AND RESTORES LIVES

———•———

A s I said in the beginning, we must expend more time and
resources preparing to prevent than preparing to react.
That means providing interventions before spending large
sums on reaction drills.

It's not my opinion that the intervention themes you'll learn in this
chapter work. It's the evidence of twelve years of application. While
you can't always prove an attack didn't happen, there are measures
of success:

- Reduction of authentic massacre threats
- Reduction of building evacuations
- Reduction of discipline/behavioral referrals
- Improvement of classroom performance

As explained earlier, Texas hadn't had a major attack since the
trend started in 1997 because many of the highest risk suburban
and small town districts used the intervention themes through 2002.
The proof of performance is self-evident. Today, though, Texas has
threats like the rest of North America because almost none of the

districts continued to apply what they learned—mainly due to staff attrition, as discussed in the last chapter.

Working with students based upon their profile isn't new; I just didn't call it that when I was in the classroom. For example, if you have a shy student, teachers know that it is better to sit or stand to the side of a student as they provide instruction. The student is more relaxed than if a teacher adopts an intimidating square-shouldered face-to-face stance over a student. For other students who like to show emotion, teachers may use more adjectives, metaphors, and descriptors than for students who are more stoic. What Korem suggests is similar: if students have the Random Actor traits, treat them respectfully based upon who they are. This is the difference he uncovered between FedEx and USPS. Now you'll learn how the same intervention themes have been used on K–12 and higher education campuses. What follows is adapted from *Rage of the Random Actor* in Dan Korem's voice.[1]

THE 3-POINT INTERVENTION ROAD MAP

The 3-point intervention works with the two Random Actor traits: the high Unconventional and high Fearful traits. The intervention first allows students to function comfortably without paranoia—usually within weeks. Then, over time, the intervention guides them out of the destructive profile so they are no longer plagued by paranoia. The three intervention themes as they relate to the two traits are as follows:

Unconventional Trait

Theme#1: Provide change, variability and flexibility in day-to-day routines, assignments, and interactions that meet the needs of the Unconventional trait. Modify classroom instruction and interactions that are stiff, autocratic, unchanging, and inflexible.

Fearful Trait

Theme #2: Provide protective factors that meet the needs of the high Fearful trait and subdue paranoia. Practical applications of this theme include protection from abuse, bullying, and isolation. In other words, promote inclusion versus exclusion, camaraderie versus antagonism, positive relationships versus bullying and taunting.

Theme #3: Mentor how to make decisions out of Confidence, which guides students out of the Random Actor profile and into the Cautious Innovator or Innovator profile.

Here is the big picture. The first two themes immediately reduce a student's agitation and rage and allow him to function in the classroom now. The short-term gains are that threats usually stop and classroom performance improves.

The third theme over time guides a student out of the destructive profile and reduces the potential for extreme rage and volatility. It is possible that a student can revert back, but most don't.

The first two themes usually produce significant results within four to six weeks. Students are more at ease, cooperative, able to focus on assignments, and are less agitated. I observed the same effect in the early 1990s at FedEx.

FedEx team leadership typically outperforms the local post office on the first two themes. There is more flexibility when working with staff and the environment is more inclusive when compared to poorly managed post offices that isolate and deride employees. Not surprisingly, about two-thirds of the Random Actor postal shooters worked inside versus outside jobs—where there is more change and variability.

In companies, mass attacks are more likely in plants with assembly lines than in art or other creative departments. There is little change and variability on the assembly line, while art departments are usually free-flowing and tasks are less repetitive. Similarly, accounting departments are more likely to have an attack than marketing and advertising.

In schools, alternative education campuses for at-risk students are more flexible teaching environments when compared to most high schools and middle schools. They have lower pupil-teacher ratios. Together this promotes more interaction, increases academic performance, and reduces fear. Protective factors are also always in place; bullying, gang attire, and ridicule are not accepted.

So the idea is to take the same proven themes and apply them on all campuses. Even campuses that can't lower the teacher-pupil ratio see immediate reduction of threats by using the themes. One of the most valuable campus assets is that educators as a group are able to quickly mentor one another in how to apply these themes for a specific student. This is because one of the charges of an educator is to help nurture students in addition to preparing their minds for the future.

There is a temptation that must be avoided. I've observed campuses that apply the first two themes—providing change and flexibility with protective factors—then stop because the campus is "now safe." While threats are now reduced, *the student will still have the Random Actor* traits. The long term goal should always be to guide him out of the profile.

One of the major differences between schools and the workplace is that students are mentored as well as educated in the classroom. As you will see, teaching students how to make small decisions out of Confidence—the third theme—is something any teacher or professor can do as a part of daily instruction. It actually takes *less* time to apply because instruction becomes easier and less taxing. This isn't a wishful opinion, but what most educators and administrators experience.

Finally, the three strategic themes should not be interpreted as a simplistic approach, as there are an infinite variety of ways they can be applied. Rather, they are behaviorally and thoughtfully appropriate. Also, appropriate diagnostic expertise and psychological and psychiatric assistance should be incorporated as required.

Who needs to know and apply the 3-point intervention and why

Teachers and professors as a group are critical—they must know how to identify the traits and how to intervene. First, they spend more time with a student and are more likely to see the traits. Second, they can apply the intervention as a normal part of daily instruction. Administrators and principals should be familiar with the intervention so they can empower staff to make decisions as needed. Counselors should understand the traits and intervention so they behaviorally support a student. Campus security should be able to identify Random Actor traits and understand how the intervention themes can be applied when interacting with students.

Mitigating risk

Although stated earlier, it must be reemphasized: Thousands of non-behavioral science professionals have learned this three-point intervention strategy. Not only have lives been positively directed, but in application, there has not been one lawsuit or letter of complaint filed. The reasons for this are the themes are common sense and they can be applied by those who don't necessarily have advanced behavioral training—excluding cases, of course, in which someone has a diagnosable condition.

Second, the medicine tastes good. The intervention comprises three thoughtful interactions that can be applied in any culture: more flexibility, protective factors, and mentoring how to make Confident decisions. So why would a student complain?

The worst case outcome is that campus staff inaccurately believes a student has the Random Actor traits and the student becomes the beneficiary of these thoughtful interactions. The student may not need additional variety or protective factors, but there's no harm done. In practical application, though, misidentification is unlikely because the Random Actor traits are *extreme* and are typically easy to identify. Since 1997, I don't know of a case of misidentification.

To mitigate risk, students are educated in an environment that doesn't inherently antagonize the two traits and doesn't inhibit classroom productivity. Then, they are mentored how to make decisions out of confidence outside their area(s) of expertise so that they move away from paranoia and out of the Random Actor profile. Now let's look at the three themes in more detail.

THEME 1: PROVIDE CHANGE, VARIABILITY, AND FLEXIBILITY

Supporting the Unconventional Trait

A person who is high Unconventional typically prefers: positive change and variety, innovative environments, the freedom to move about without restraint. When working with a student, ask yourself if what you are applying is a fit for the above.

Extreme Random Actors can be offended by confinement, minimal change, severe repetition, autocratic directives, and authority without compassion.

What follows is a case in which the right questions weren't asked. A well-intentioned teacher had a Random Actor student in her class who was struggling. She wanted to help, but did the *opposite* of what was needed. When I polled educators and school administrators on the 10th anniversary of the Columbine massacre *over two-thirds chose the same incorrect instructional style.* This has been consistent since 1997 when we first started training teachers. For them, this was an "aha!" moment. Corporate executives who were polled fared just as poorly.

After the teacher completed our training, she lamented that she knew of many teachers who made the same mistake. Here is what she told me.

I've taught kids who had the Random Actor traits, but at the time I really didn't know how to describe what I saw. These kids usually seemed a bit out of sorts, less disciplined, even if they weren't overly disruptive. My natural inclination was to have them sit next to a student who had the Manager traits — someone who was efficient and could set a positive example. Now I realize that this was exactly what I *shouldn't* have done. I should have had a student with the Unconventional trait who was a Cautious Innovator or Innovator seated next to that student or work with him on a project. It's sort of obvious now why there was such a disconnect. One was Unconventional and the other was Conventional. . . . and I was trying to do the right thing. I've watched some of the other teachers do exactly the same thing.

As discussed earlier, people with the Random Actor traits often inherently dislike individuals, locations, and environments that represent the Manager quadrant. This is because the Manager has

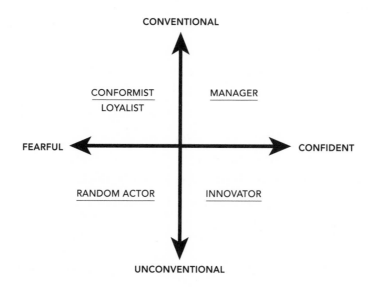

the *opposite* traits of the Random Actor.

If the student in this teacher's class had a high Conventional trait, then perhaps a positive role-model student with a Conventional trait would be the right person to sit next to this student. But, in this case, a disciplined student with the Unconventional trait would be a better match—an Innovator. Does this mean that there must always be a "trait match?" No, as there might be other factors, like a prior positive relationship, that makes sense. But a person who is Unconventional or at least low Conventional and more naturally spontaneous, unconventional, etc. is a better choice to pair with the Random Actor traits.

The idea here is that Unconventional students are *more* likely to be productive and *less* hostile if they are on a campus that doesn't inherently and unnecessarily aggravate them. Alternative education teachers and administrators regularly observe that their schools have fewer discipline problems, and their Random Actor students are more productive than in traditional classrooms. In these schools, change and variability are second nature for these professionals; they are always willing to try something new to connect with their kids, and their students usually respond positively. Even though there are *more* rules in an alternative school, they are administered with compassion and make students feel safer, thus their paranoia is less likely to be agitated—the third strategic theme.

Common sense solutions for working with the Unconventional trait are the key. Thankfully, as any administrator can tell you, if a specific teacher has trouble coming up with a creative idea, there are two more who can. Once team members understand the basic theme of what is needed, creative solutions follow.

This doesn't mean that a person with the Random Actor traits can't learn to operate with constraints or perform repetitive tasks without considering them antagonistic. In fact, it can be a healthy exercise for students with a high Unconventional trait to learn to operate for periods of time in a more Conventional environment and broaden their *range* of tolerance. But, over time, in a daily routine, the wise leader will find ways to vary responsibilities, assignments and "scenery," and pair with those who are more Unconventional or at least low Conventional.

Examples of Teaching and Leading Students

Paul Trull, a tall distinguished looking chap, is the superintendent of schools in Paris, Texas, a community of about 25,000 with 4,000 students. In 2000, his staff was trained how to apply the interventions and he hasn't had a building evacuation in nine years. After a day of Random Actor violence prevention training with his 300-plus educators, Paul came to the front, thanked everyone for their enthusiastic participation, and then said: "I kind of like what Dan has shared with us, don't you?"

As he recapped the high points of what they learned, he removed his jacket and loosened his tie. Then, he pulled out a shirt tail, and tousled his thick, immaculately combed silver hair. It was *so* out of character. Looking every part the Innovator to the laughter of his staff district, they got the message.

"I know I kind of like this idea about how to approach and treat some of our kids," he added. Paul demonstrated that even the most *managerish* can loosen up a bit when interacting with a Random Actor youth.

The role of an executive officer in a school or system is to set a tone by example—especially superintendents who oversee a school district/system and school principals who lead staffs. In higher education it's the deans, presidents and chancellors who set the tone. They may not actually work with students, but they lead by example. For executives who are Managers, demonstrating flexibility for staff is a key ingredient to reduce the potential for setting off the paranoia of a student with the Random Actor traits.

Another example of a leader who set aside his Manager façade is Phil Warrick—who was honored as Nebraska's outstanding new principal in 1998. He started a program to reach at-risk youth that can be especially effective reaching Random Actor students. In his own words:

> It is a simple concept really, but gives me the chance to profile students who have gotten in trouble. It works like this: Any student who gets put into an in-school suspension situation eats lunch with the administrators that day. We usually go into a separate area where no other people are and have a really relaxed lunch together. While we are eating we try and talk about times we got into trouble as kids or we get the students involved in discussions about their home life or love life or even gang affiliations, if they are willing to talk about it. And as you are aware, they like to talk about it. Our goals is to build some small bridges and break down the 'authority wall' [Manager wall] that can get built up with kids. This program, though simple, has paid big dividends. Some days we bring in pizza and the kids go nuts. One day we brought in pizza and a kid got up to throw his lunch away, and I said, 'Hey, let me throw that lunch away for you' . . . he just roared as I slam dunked his lunch into the trash. I will take more time this year to profile the students using your ideas as we eat lunch together.

When leaders lead, staff is then empowered to do what they do best: educate. During one workshop I asked the elementary school teachers to come up with some outside-the-box options for assignments that could win over a student with the Random Actor traits and help them elevate academically. Within minutes, they whipped up the assignment shown on the next page. Students are given the option of which assignment they would like to work on related to shapes. The Conventional assignment focus (top one) asks a student to count the number of squares. For Unconventional

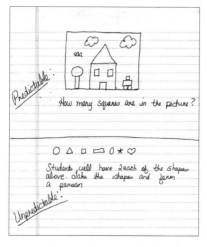

Predictable

How many squares are in the picture?

○ △ □ ▱ 0 ✦ ♡

Students will have each of the shapes above. Take the shapes and form a person.

Unpredictable.

option, a student who prefers less constraint, could assemble the shapes to make a person.

In an affluent community, after a day of training, an inspired educator created this "Innovator At Work" poster. It had the same positive flavor as another poster created and posted by a school counselor in her office. It read: "When you come into this office we will respect you, listen carefully, do what we can, and maybe even give you a hug. So Get Used To It!"

One of the most stressful Manager events on campuses is preparing for and administering standardized testing. In many K–12 schools, students endure weeks and weeks of Manager-style drills to help prepare for the tests. Even outside-the-box schools can become fill-in-the box compression chambers for students. This results in Random Actor threats that are regularly set

DON'T SHOOT

INNOVATOR
AT WORK

off across the United States. This is a strategic time to apply more change, variability, and flexibility in the entire preparation and test taking process.

The director of education for a leading suburban school system wrote an enthusiastic appraisal of what he learned after his district was trained to apply the intervention themes. In his review, though, he forcefully noted the intolerable level of stress in his district on

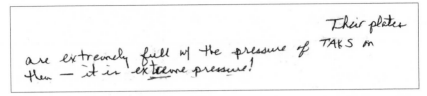

Their plates are extremely full w/ the pressure of TAKS on them — it is 'extreme pressure!

teachers while preparing for testing, as shown on the next page. When teachers are in the pressure cooker for weeks and weeks, individual attention to students evaporates. All students are more stressed. And a common result is students with the Random Actor traits acting out and making threats.

Campus security and law enforcement can activate the theme of providing more flexibility to reduce the Manager wall and solicit cooperation and to prevent violence.

"Deputy Don" was a student resource officer (SRO) in a high school in the wealthy suburb of West Palm Beach, Florida, home of the PGA (Professional Golfer's Association). The dress code in his school prohibited the wearing of choker collars or arm bands that have spikes. One day, a frumpy and stuffy principal, tartly told him to bring the student in to her office because he refused to listen to her. Don, who exudes an Innovator flair, approached the student and asked him if he would please give him the collar. The student responded, "I'll give it to you, but I won't give it to that old b----.'"

Don also suspected that he might have a gun in his possession and that he was capable of using it. Stepping outside, where they couldn't be seen, Don searched him and found a pack of cigarettes.

"After talking to him for a little while, he finally told me if I let him have a cigarette he would take me to the 'damn gun.' I told him to light up. I recovered the gun and quite a few bullets, and he was the type of student who would use it."

It is important for campus officers to have the ability to change their appearance and procedure to create more of an Innovator façade when confronting Random Actor students. This not only includes quick modifications in the uniform, but also flexibility in their approach. Don's confrontation in this case was a little more extreme, but he consistently demonstrated sound judgment, got along with the students and faculty, and helped thwart crime before it even got started.

Regarding other strategies for reducing crime, anecdotally, some schools that have school uniforms have a lower crime rate. Everyone is on an even plane, and it levels out the visual distinction between the haves and have-nots. However, if a community decides that uniforms are appropriate, it is advisable to provide some change and variety in the uniforms and to stress this factor to youths with the Random Actor traits.

THEME 2: PUT PROTECTIVE FACTORS IN PLACE

Protective Factors for the Fearful Trait

Anyone who feels unsafe or threatened could lash out at the source of a threat or do something irrational. For the Random Actor, though, responding irrationally is more likely than for others because of the high Fearful trait. To mitigate this kind of irrational behavior, it only makes sense to provide protective factors that make students feel safe.

For the last ten years, education professionals have noted that bullying is becoming a greater problem in public schools. It's hard to quantify and prove that bullying measured on a per capita/incident basis is greater now than say in the 1950s. Recent Random Actor school massacres, killings, and plots are unique in North American and European history as a trend, and many of these youths complained that they were being picked on or bullied by others. This doesn't justify violence, but it is a fact.

For Luke, bullying by his mother and classmates was a major factor that touched off his rage. His mother regularly berated him with misplaced blame for causing her failed marriage, and he was often taunted by students. In the absence of any protective factors, this intensified his isolation and made him easy to recruit into Boyette's self-styled Kroth gang where he was given the promise of occultic power over those who troubled him.

In a noteworthy case in 1993, two 10-year-old boys in Liverpool England killed a 2-year-old boy, James Bolger, whom they lured out of a shopping mall. After killing young James with rocks, they put his body on train tracks where it was severed in two by an oncoming train. The boys were the youngest ever convicted of murder in English legal history.

Det. Supt. Albert Kirby of the Liverpool City Police Force directed the investigation. When one of the boys was brought in to be interviewed, within minutes, the young lad, unprompted, talked about being bullied at school. Here is a brief excerpt from his confession.

Haunting image: A shopping center's security camera recorded James Bolger, foreground, being led away by an older boy in February 1993.

Q: How long have you been at Walton St. Mary's?

A: A year I think, two years, I don't know.

Q: What's it like there?

A: All right.

Q: Are you happy at school?

A: Yeah, sometimes, but people bully me.

Q: Do they?

A: Yeah.

Q: Who bullies you?

A: The lads.

Both he and the other boy, who was the leader, came from broken homes and both exhibited the extreme Random Actor traits. In light of the significant number of Random Actor youths in schools, policy backed by thoughtful action that discourages bullying is prudent; it reduces irrational behavior and the possibility of one youth destructively directing another.

One myth that currently persists, though, is that bullying by itself sparks mass attacks. This is inaccurate. If you bully students who don't have the Random Actor traits, they may strike out at the bully, but they won't irrationally kill everyone else around them.

The recipe for disaster is when a student with the Random Actor traits is bullied, mercilessly belittled, marginalized, and isolated. Then you might get a combustible reaction.

Here is an example where a principal from a small town in Wisconsin describes how she intervened on behalf of a Random Actor youth who was being bullied.

Incident that occurred during the 1998–99 school year where I was the principal:

- 9th grade male in art class was being bullied by a senior male athlete. First, verbally ("I heard you had sex with your mother.") then physically (shoving).
- 9th grader's response was verbal ("I'll bring a gun and shoot you."). Also, made motions of using art tools to cut self.

Actions taken were:

- Changed the 9th grader's art class by shuffling the schedule [so athlete wasn't in same class].
- Identified a male teacher who was known as an adult who could build rapport with kids easily and had him make contact with the student on an ongoing basis about interests of the student (basketball).
- Found a "job" for the student that would help him become a member of the school and have prestige/importance

(videotaped girls' basketball games).

The paranoia of the student was immediately reduced by directly addressing stressors—the bullying athlete. An educator/coach then provided the one-on-one dialogue that again reduced the student's paranoia. She then made sure her student had a creative contributory role in the school so that he wasn't isolated and that met the needs of his Unconventional trait—videotaping girls' basketball games.

Note in this case that the student threatened to create a self-inflicted wound. Most Random Actor attackers threaten or do commit suicide. Briefly, in non-urban educated communities like suburbs and small towns, student suicide rates are often significantly higher than in urban communities. (For a detailed discussion on this, see *Rage of the Random Actor*.)

Luke threatened suicide after he was apprehended by Pearl Police and was placed on a suicide watch. Although he told Bill Dodson there wasn't anything that could have been done to have prevented the attack, it's clear that had protective factors been applied, it would have defused Luke's rage, which most likely would have resulted in a different outcome.

THEME 3: COACH HOW TO MAKE CONFIDENT DECISIONS

This third theme or intervention guides a student out of the Random Actor profile and takes place during natural day-to-day interactions and assignments. Students are mentored how to make tiny, bite-sized decisions out of confidence *outside their area of expertise and core competence.*

Remember, making Confident decisions in an area of expertise is not the same as making Confident decisions in everyday experiences. In other words, we're not looking at how confidently students complete assignments in a class in which they naturally excel, but how do they handle making decisions when faced with rejection, a

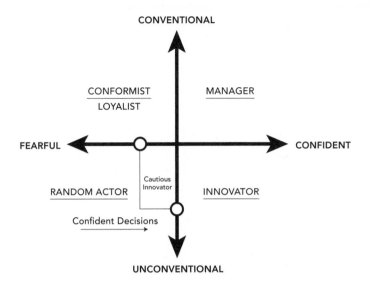

set-back, working with someone they don't relate to, etc.

With the repetition of small Confident decisions, most K–12 students within weeks move away from paranoia—the extreme end of the Fearful trait into the Cautious Innovator, as shown in this graph. Here, students make decisions out of caution, which isn't inherently harmful. Their extreme volatility dissipates. For young adult students in higher education, this process may take longer.

The Cautious Innovator quadrant isn't inherently volatile like the Random Actor quadrant. Here a student prefers to do things that are different, outside-the-box, unconventional, etc. but may need time to process a decision because he or she is cautious, which is fine.

If a student doesn't move to the Confident side of the gauge that's OK, although with increasingly Confident decisions, many do move into the Innovator quadrant. What is most important is that they are no longer tethered by paranoia and realize they have direct control over their well-being and destiny.

The result: The ability to make decisions out of increased confidence, as a strength they have direct control over—what many Random Actor protest they don't have.

THE ANSWER TO THE MOST IMPORTANT QUESTION

Of the two Random Actor traits, the high Fearful trait is the agitating trait that triggers violent Random Actor acts. So the obvious question is:

If making decisions out of Fear/Paranoia is what makes an extreme Random Actor potentially destructive or even dangerous, what is the antidote?

Ask a group of educators and parents this question, and the typical responses are: *Make them feel more confident. Take away their fear.*

The problem is that we can't make students more confident or less fearful when making decisions because this is an act of their will. Confidence is something that is an earned character trait, and not something that can be artificially inserted. It's like exercising a muscle in the psyche and will. Use it and it grows and strengthens. Don't use it and it withers and shrinks.

So if you're an educator or parent or care-giver, *specifically* what do you do? As the question is a simple one, so too is the answer:

We help a student learn to make decisions out of Confidence.

This is not an intervention we *do* for a person, but rather something where we provide *guidance*. It starts with small, bite-sized decisions.

For an elementary student, here are typical decisions they can make. Bring their pencils to class for the next two days. Don't hang out with Alex on the playground for *three days* because he's not a good influence.

For a high school student: study 10 minute more on algebra for one week; work with a student he is uncomfortable with on a project for one day.

For a college student: participate in a class discussion at least once in the next week; study two more hours a week instead of hanging out or going to a party.

There isn't a formula for identifying the best decisions for each student because their needs, interests, studies, environment, and so on are different. Experience demonstrates, though, that educators and administrators who interact with a student the basic themes will identify what will work.

A common-sense, six-step process will help students make the right decisions—strengthening their decision-making muscle. I will briefly review those steps here and provide an example of an intervention with a student in the next chapter. Some students will quickly go through the process, while others may require months to progress. A general rule of thumb is that for ages 10 through the early 20s, one can undertake the first five steps within a matter of weeks. For older subjects, the process can take weeks to months. For both age groups, it is the minority who won't respond at all or are unable to do so without psychiatric or special care.

1. Develop trust. For a student to follow your guidance there must be some level of trusting communication. This can take hours or months to establish. For youth, it usually occurs within a shorter time than for an young adult—even as short as one meeting.

2. Seek acknowledgment that they make decisions out of extreme Fear. At some point, students must recognize that thhe make Fear-based decisions in areas outside of their competency. I have respondents plot themselves on a 0–5 scale, with 5 being high Fearful. This is important in part so that they take ownership of the process. But, even more important, when they acknowledge this problem, they are making a decision out of confidence to trust someone else.

3. Seek acknowledgment that they don't want to continue to live in Fear. If students don't want to change, there isn't much one can do. Deep down, most people who operate out of paranoia, though, desire to be rid of this demon. They must clearly and convincingly acknowledge that they don't want to make decisions out of extreme fear. This doesn't mean that they will immediately be able to do it—rather, there is at least the desire to begin.

4. Help them decide on a Confident decision they can make that day. Once they decide that they want to change, right there, on the spot, some kind of decision should be made regarding something they control. Here are qualifications for an appropriate decision:

- Concrete—not abstract
- Nugget-sized
- Time-compacted (for an immediate result)
- Specific—not expansive
- Short duration—not drawn out

The idea is to help students decide on an immediate Confident decision over which they have control and which has quick closure. Just "doing better in algebra" is vague, general, and not time-compacted. Spending ten minutes more on homework assignments for a week is a better decision.

Also, it's best if *students* come up with the decision. Offering them a list of tasks does not offer them *control* of the process—it puts *you* in control, which can be part of the problem. You act only as a guiding sounding board. They must wrestle with the idea and how it directly applies to their life. This ensures that they internalize what is happening and take ownership.

5. Weekly, if not daily, provide encouragement and guidance to make simple, time-compacted decisions out of Confidence. Each week new decisions must be selected and acted upon.

6. Over time, encourage them to make decisions that are more challenging, complex, and take longer to complete. As students move away from the extreme of paranoia to cautious decision making, decisions should become more challenging and take longer.

A simple, time-compacted decision in the beginning might be: Work with Mary (something he dislikes) on the project for a day. A more challenging decision might be: Work with Mary for two weeks and find at least two positive things you like about her. Again, there is no set list of suggestions for more complex decisions—rather, just be guided by common sense, feedback from the student, insight from your colleagues, etc.

STRATEGIC CONSIDERATIONS FOR APPLYING THE 3-POINT INTERVENTION

The most common intervention mistake is that campus administrators rely solely upon the intervention team to identify students in trouble without providing training for teachers. It is critical to recognize that *teachers are the most important part of the equation because they spend more time with the students than anyone and are best suited to identify the Random Actor traits.*

Here is a typical outcome in an extremely high-risk charter school in New Jersey. Alice Guy, a board member of the Washington, D.C., Association of Threat Assessment Professionals provided Random Actor training in 2006 for faculty where there were five to six threats a week against life and limb. Here are the results she reported to the state board of education:

> This training was funded through the New Jersey Department of Education, on a grant for violence prevention programs. The initial result is that last year, the administrator received an average of 5-6 disciplinary notices from teachers about students each week involving specific threats by a student to hurt or kill another student. While basic altercations still take place (you cut in front of me in line; you stole my pencil) the *serious* threats are just not happening. They've gone from several each week prior to the training to zero

after the training. . . . There had not been a student threat to kill or harm another student from September 2006 through the end of the school year. The head administrator plans to take this information to the state.

If I have a regret, it's that I didn't know about this research while I was the superintendent at Pearl. Korem had trained over 50 professionals in Pearl in 1999—mental health, law enforcement, hostage negotiators and a few from our district at the request of local law enforcement—but I never met him. We briefly connected in 2000 in Houston, and later spent a good bit of time together at the Association of Community College Trustees convention in 2005 where he gave an address on his research.

Luke Woodham was a student with the Random Actor profile who was nurtured in our school in what we considered to be a safe environment. What I now know is that we could have intervened—and probably averted the tragedy at our school. But we did not.

If you live in a suburb or small town like mine, please don't be lulled to inaction by the calm pastoral scene outside your window. Unfortunately all our campuses today have students with the Random Actor profile. They need our help. Intervention is an investment that is worth the modest cost of time and resources required to provide aid to students who think taking someone else's life and possibly their own is a solution to whatever is troubling them.

In education, both K–12 and higher education, we are known as a profession where we tend to jump to the newest flavor of the month. Don't let this be the case when it comes to preventing Random Actor attacks. On the walls of your campus corridors are fire extinguishers to put out fires. They are visible, regularly charged, and always ready for use. Do the same with what you learn in this book. If you're an administrator, provide the concepts to your staff, be sure they use them, and provide what is necessary to sustain protection and assistance.

CHAPTER 10

THE WAY OUT...

———•———

The following case is a composite case of an intervention from Dan Korem's files.[1] It shows us how to guide a student toward confident decisions.

Most would agree that teenagers are potentially more volatile than adults as a group. It is easier to get them to commit a violent irrational act than someone in their 40s, which is why they are often targeted for recruitment as suicide terrorists. That's what makes the case of "Tony" in this chapter so remarkable. He's a compilation of three youths, to protect identities, who hailed from various ethnic and cultural backgrounds in an upscale suburb.

Korem applied the six-step intervention detailed in the last chapter, and within weeks "Tony" was no longer making decisions out of paranoia, his rage dissipated, he ceased making threats, and his poor performance at school improved. Over the following months, he moved from the Random Actor quadrant into the Cautious Innovator or Innovator quadrants as he learned how to make decisions out of confidence.

Korem provides the following dialogue, which is very close to the original interactions, and is similar to dialogue used by others who have applied the six-step process.

BACKGROUND

Tony, who had been arrested on drug charges, was known to carry a pistol at various times, and had contemplated compiling a "hit list" of students he didn't like. He agreed to talk to Korem at the urging of some students he knew. Tony also knew Korem's two sons, Erik (14) and Luke (12), who brought him home one day after school. Korem asked his boys to join him at his kitchen table so they could see first-hand how to help someone like Tony if he wasn't around. Also, when Erik was young, he was a bit overweight. Today, he's a strength and conditioning coach, but when he was young, kids would occasionally pick on him because of his weight, and Tony knew this.

While alternative education professionals will tell you that it usually takes no more than 2–4 weeks to go through this process with a student, Korem was able to go through the first five steps in one afternoon—about two hours—because Tony knew and trusted him. Where needed, amplification or clarification is provided in brackets.

1. Develop Trust.

DK: Tony, some of your friends asked me to get together with you. I know you've been struggling a bit and they thought I could help. Do you mind if I ask you a couple of questions?

Tony: Sure.

[Tony was hesitant and had trouble making sustained eye contact, but because he had some positive prior interactions with me, he opened up after about half an hour. He also knew that I was street savvy and wouldn't be shocked by anything he told me. Care, concern, patience, love, candor when appropriate, and a non-judgmental attitude about doing what is right is the rudder to gaining someone's trust in a mentoring relationship. Tony was headed down the wrong path and I wouldn't hesitate to point this out without berating him, and he accepted this because he knew that I cared about him.]

2. Tony must acknowledge that he makes decisions out of extreme fear.

DK: You've known Erik for a while. Do you think he makes decisions out of confidence?

Tony: Yeah.

DK: Now don't tell me that because he's sitting here and he's my son. How do you know that?

Tony: Well, when he was younger the kids used to pick on him and even though he was stronger than them, he never took them out [beat them up].

DK: Are you like that? I mean, are you pretty good at making confident decisions?

Tony: Not really.

DK: Do you ever wonder whether people like you or not?

Tony: What do you mean?

DK: I'm not talking about you wondering about what kids think because you have a new pimple on your face or because you don't know if kids will like what you're wearing. [He laughed.] I'm talking about you always kind of looking over your shoulder wondering if people like you or not.

Tony: Yeah, kind of.

[He's hesitant here because this is uncomfortable.]

DK: Or, when you get up in the morning, can you look in the mirror and say, "No matter whether I succeed or fail, I know that I'll give this day everything I've got." Can you do that?

Tony: Nah, I don't think so.

DK: Now of the two, who do you like better, Michael Jordan [who is extremely confident] or Dennis Rodman [known for his outrageous behavior and paranoia]?

Tony: Rodman [smiles]!

[I used this question in the 1990s with kids because if they were high FEARFUL, they usually didn't like Jordan because he was CONFIDENT. Jordan had something—CONFIDENT decision making—they didn't have and it made them resentful/hostile.]

DK: So, what is it about Rodman that you like, instead of Jordan?

[We talked this through, and after we got past that Rodman is "different," he eventually acknowledged that it wasn't that he liked Rodman more, rather he *didn't* like Jordan because of his confidence, and it made him uneasy.]

DK: You know how you said that you're always wondering if people like you or not? And, how it's hard to look at things confidently? How would you like to get a little of that off your back? So it doesn't drag you down all the time? [At this stage, individualized dialogue and probing is required, but the goal is for them to buy in to the idea that they want to change, even though they don't know or understand what is required for them to do to change.]

Tony: Yeah, if I could.

DK: Well, on a scale of 0 to 5, how fearful do you think you are when making decisions if 0 is low FEARFUL and 5 is high FEARFUL.

[Here, amplified dialogue is necessary to articulate and reinforce what is meant by FEARFUL decisions outside the area of one's competence. In this case, Tony circled "5" on a hand-drawn linear scale. This is very powerful, not only because Tony has taken ownership of the concept and internalized it, but more important, he has made a decision out of CONFIDENCE to trust someone with sensitive information. For Tony, it was the first time in his life that he actually verbalized this to himself or anyone else.]

3. Tony must acknowledge that he doesn't want to continue to live in FEAR.

DK: Do you always want to stay on the high FEARFUL side? Always having to look over your shoulder? Never feeling at ease? Wouldn't you like to get just a little of this off your back? [Expansive and relevant dialogue is required here. Tony said he didn't understand what it would be like to make CONFIDENT decisions. The first time this idea/option is presented, it's not uncommon for someone's eyes to almost glaze over, as if disoriented or lost in thought. It took about an hour before he grasped the idea. For some, this idea can take several discussions over a period of several weeks.]

DK: Would you like to at least be just a little fearful and get that monkey off your back?

Tony: Yeah, if it really works.

[Note that you avoid statements like, *You don't want to*

live in fear the rest of your life, rather this is a participatory process where you ask questions. If a person is going to truly change, it requires internalizing and thinking through what is required.]

DK: Well, what do you think it would feel like if you did that? What would it feel like not to be hounded by your own fear? Have you seen anybody that has done that?

[The idea is to stimulate his thinking so he can eventually articulate what this change might look and feel like, rather than just telling him what it will be like. Other useful questions are: Can you remember a time when you made a confident decision? What was it? What happened? How did you make it? Did it help you? Would you like to make more decisions like that?]

DK: So how are you going to move from high FEARFUL to at least low FEARFUL or even CONFIDENT? How would you do that?

[Using the gauge drawn on a piece of paper, point to exactly what you are talking about as this is an abstract concept. For Tony, we talked about the difference between Jordan—on the CONFIDENT side—and what he did that was different from Rodman on the FEARFUL side.]

Tony: Well, Rodman has to have all those tattoos and body piercings to be something . . . and Jordan doesn't. He feels good enough about himself not to have to put all that stuff on.

[While tattoos and body piercings don't necessarily mean a person is FEARFUL, Tony recognized that for Rodman these were only "props" used to pretend that he was something that he wasn't—it was a distraction that people focused on, rather than the Rodman inside.]

DK: You said that Erik was confident when he made decisions. Who do you know who isn't like Erik and makes decisions out of fear?

Tony: Jason's like that. He's always putting people down, but I know that's because he's insecure.

[The idea is to have Tony articulate from his perspective who is and isn't CONFIDENT when making decisions, with specific examples to ensure that he understands the concept. My participation simply helped guide him in the right direction and if necessary challenged or corrected examples or ideas that weren't on target.]

DK: So, what do you think that you have to do to move out of this high FEARFUL area when making decisions?

[This is an extremely important juncture. Here, Tony must articulate that he has to make decisions out of confidence. Simply "being confident" isn't specific enough. He must literally articulate, without being told, that he is the one who must begin making decisions out of confidence. When he grasps this idea, then you can move forward to the *kind* of decisions he should start making. This is a patient, guided process that Tony himself must struggle with and internalize the bottom line action he needs to take. It might take several discussions to get to this point without spoon-feeding him the idea. Once he specifically articulates *I have to make decisions out of confidence*, then we can move on to the next step.]

4. Help Tony decide on a CONFIDENT decision he can make that day.

DK: So what is going to be your first decision that you can make today?

Tony: I'll do better in algebra.

[Stated after reflection.]

DK: That won't work. It's too vague. Come up with something better.

[At this point Tony is guided to pick a decision that meets
the criteria noted in the last chapter. The decision must
be:

- Concrete—not abstract
- Nugget-sized
- Time-compacted (for an immediate result)
- Specific—not expansive
- Short duration—not drawn out]

Tony: I won't wear my silver choker [necklace] to school for a
week.

DK: What does that have to do with confident decision making?

[This should be probed carefully to be sure he has the
right cause and effect relationship.]

Tony: I use them as my props to get people to like me?

DK: So, you think that's a CONFIDENT decision that you could
do today?

Tony: Yeah. I wear them because I want people to like me.

DK: Do you think you could go to school without them and
you could get people to like you?

Tony: I don't know.

DK: Do you think it would be a good thing if you tried
that?

Tony: Yeah.

DK: Would it be a little scary?

Tony: Yeah.

DK: Do you think that would be a decision out of confidence?

Tony: Yeah.

[Removing a piece of jewelry may not be an appropriate decision for everyone, but Tony realized he used his jewelry to prop himself up like Rodman. He took ownership of his situation, made an honest appraisal, and an act of character followed. Does this mean that he should never wear jewelry? No. Once he realizes that he doesn't need jewelry to move forward in life, then he can choose to wear it again, which is what happened. One can't stereotype the specific decisions someone should or shouldn't make, rather the decisions should be appropriate for that person at that point in time.]

5. Weekly, if not daily, provide encouragement and guidance so Tony makes simple, time-compacted decisions out of Confidence.

Weekly, I encouraged Tony to make another decision. At school, teachers do this as a part of instruction. In an organization, this can be a weekly part of on-the-job mentoring. And then there are other impromptu situations where it makes sense to encourage an on-the-spot decision. One day Tony came over to the house, and he was severely agitated. Here is what happened:

Tony: Mr. Korem, we need to talk. I mean really need to talk.

DK: Sure. What is it?

Tony: Did you hear about that kid last night who almost had his eyes torn out of his head? Man, I'm scared . . . I know some of those kids.

[Rival gang members from a skinhead gang, The Third Power, got in a fight with a sports gang called the Moostangs, a twist on the school mascot, the Mustangs, at a Richardson high school—this, in a Dallas suburb that at the time was statistically the safest city in Texas and the 17th safest city in the United States with a population of more than 100,000. The most common youth gang in Europe is a football (soccer) hooligan gang. There are a variety of these gangs that attach themselves to football clubs and do battle with gangs that follow competing clubs sometimes even resulting in deaths. The student in the Moostangs tried to use a technique taught to soldiers for hand-to-hand combat where one takes the thumbs and drives them into the brain to kill. The youth, whose vision was permanently impaired, came to my son Erik's football game with a T-shirt that read, "An eye for an eye." After Tony and I talked through the situation and he calmed down, I noticed some rubber bands on his wrist.]

DK: Say, Tony, what are those rubber bands on your wrist?
[He had about twenty on his right wrist. Anytime I see something new in the youth subculture, I always ask kids what it's all about. Some kids wear them to cover the slash marks on their wrists; while not always suicidal, many kids today are "cutters" and are involved in self-mutilation, which can be a foreshadowing of suicidal tendencies. Sheepishly, Tony knew what was coming next when he told me why he wore them.]

Tony: I wear it as my good luck charm when I run track.

DK: Oh really . . .

Tony: Yeah, I know I shouldn't be wearing them.

DK: Why is that?

Tony: I'm not making decisions out of confidence.

DK: So what are you going to do about it?
[I was surprised that he actually had been thinking about this in great detail.]

Tony: I've thought about memorizing a verse from the Bible each week to help me.

DK: Like what verses from the Bible.

[Over time and once trust is established, it's okay to press someone if you think they're just trying to pacify you to get you off their decision-making treadmill. I wanted to be certain he wasn't just trying to con me because he knew our family attended church. But, Tony was serious.]

Tony: Well, coach quoted a verse from the second book of Timothy that says: "For God didn't give us a spirit of fear, but a spirit of power, of love, and of self-discipline."

[I was amazed. He had not only been thinking about moving away from fear-based to confident-based decisions, but he also realized he needed to be more disciplined, a potential negative action of the Unconventional trait.]

6. Over time, encourage Tony to make decisions that are more challenging, complex, and that take longer to complete.

About six months into the process, I challenged Tony to do something that I knew would stretch him. He was at 3–4 FEARFUL and on his way to the CAUTIOUS INNOVATOR type when I approached him with a tougher and more complex decision. Although he was doing better, he was having more difficulty at home, where his parents were struggling and eventually divorced. Significantly, though, he was no longer a potential threat to himself or others even though the social landscape deteriorated. In this context, I presented him with a really difficult decision.

DK: Tony, I want you to think about doing something for me.

Tony: What?

DK: I want you to come down to the mission church where Mrs. Korem and I do volunteer work [in the Dallas inner-city]. I want you to talk to the kids there about how you've learned how to make confident decisions. They come from some pretty difficult neighborhoods and it's tough every day for them.

Tony: I don't know.

DK: I think you have something to say that could really help these kids.

Tony: I don't know, Mr. Korem . . .

DK: Well, just think about it and let me know. You know when we've learned how to leave a dark place, we have a responsibility to help others do the same.

It took him a while, but several months later, Tony agreed. He was naturally nervous and apprehensive, but once he started talking, he extended well past his fifteen-minute commitment. I thought this would be a good thing for Tony for several reasons. First, it would take the focus off of his troubles and use what he learned for someone else's benefit. Second, looking into the eyes of other troubled kids would cause him to think about his personal situation and motivate him to move beyond his current circumstances it so it didn't remain a liability. Third, as he watched how they received what he shared, it reinforced for him that he was on the right path.

As already mentioned, Tony is a compilation of kids, but their stories are real. Today, none are as extremely volatile as they were when they started, but all have their own personal struggles. Usually, most kids like Tony will struggle with individual issues for twenty years or longer into their adult life. This doesn't mean, however, they can't lead a fulfilled life and make a contribution.

One Tony is now married, has a child, and works hard. He still calls and we still talk about next steps. When pressed, they more often lean to the good than that which harms. Is it possible for someone to regress? Yes, as it is for anyone with any profile to fall into bad habits and destructive behavior. But, my experience is that those who have fought their way out of the extreme FEARFUL trait don't return.

CHAPTER 11

FEDS, BULLYING, AND THE MISSING PROTECTOR STRATEGY

———•———

S oon after the 1997–1998 Random Actor school attacks, remedies such as crisis drills were promoted by those who thought the schools should practice how they would react when a tragedy occurred. On the state level, Alaska, Kentucky, and Washington first held school safety summits during summer sessions to talk about crisis management. Promoters charged an average fee of $1500 to $2000 to conduct the drills.

The idea was to visualize an angry person walking into the school such as the principal's office carrying a weapon. The school officials were told to back away calmly and proceed into a campus lock-down drill. Someone would give a coded signal over the PA system to tell the teachers to immediately secure their doors, shut the blinds, huddle the children on the floor, and tell them to be silent. It was reasoned that if the halls were cleared, the police could more easily pinpoint the location of the suspect. The campus lock-down is meant to minimize the possible targets.

Many argued that this new brand of safety drill was a waste of school dollars and some called it a case of made-to-order moral panic. According to the National School Safety Center the number of school violent deaths decreased 27 per cent from the late 1990s to 2000. This correlates with Dan Korem's research that found Random Actor attacks and threats were increasing as violent juvenile crimes was *decreasing*. But there was little focus on the increasing threats, near attacks, or how to effectively stop them. As earlier noted, Korem estimates that right before Columbine, there were 25–50 threats per day. By 2009, that number increased to 75–100 per day. At the end of the 2008–2009 school year the number was right at 100 per day. This is in addition to the thousands of threats in the weeks following the Columbine and 9/11 attacks. Other than Korem's research, I never heard of a viable explanation for these threats.

Vincent Schiraldi, the director of Justice Policy Institute, said that because there weren't large numbers of campus murders that funds should be spent increasing the ranks of counselors and adding conflict-resolution classes. He also said laws to restrict gun sales to less than one purchase a month could have a significant impact. My question is how the latter would deter a bombing attack, which was planned at Columbine and is now a common part of the equation.

In short, there are many opinions and approaches regarding the issue of school safety. Another idea floated by some was campus fortification with wire fences built around their campus with an entrance gate and armed guards posted. Other theories were advanced in major presentations at the national education administrative organizations such as the American Association of School Administrators and National Association of Secondary School Principals.

Conferences and Federal Studies

The first White House conferences took place after the Random Actor attacks that followed ours in Paducah, Kentucky; Jonesboro, Arkansas; Edinboro, Pennsylvania; and Springfield, Oregon. The

Clinton administration said it was committed to find solutions to the attacks. The first conference was held on September 1, 1998, and the second six weeks later on October 15, 1998. President Bill Clinton said he felt a special closeness to the suffering inflicted because one of the attacks, committed by a ten- and an eleven-year-old, took place in his home state of Arkansas, where he had been governor.

I represented Pearl at the first White House conference— accompanied by our mayor, Jimmy Foster, and our police chief Bill Slade, and other school administrators from our district. In attendance were school representatives from school districts who had been affected by school violence since our incident in October 1997. We shared similar stories of grief and sorrow and the discussions helped us cope with our individual situations and gave us hope for the future.

The second White House Conference was more formal, with direct participation by President Clinton, his wife Hillary, and other governmental officials. We heard from Vice President Al Gore, Secretary of Education Richard Riley, Attorney General Janet Reno and Mr. and Mrs. James Brady.

One of the highlights of the speeches was by the mother of 11-year-old Brittheny Varner, one of the children who was killed in the Jonesboro Middle School attack. She poignantly asked why a young child would want to kill another child. Her question was pondered by all of us at length. She spoke against gun access in our nation and especially against the problems it creates with our youth. Knowing that she did not speak from any political affiliation made her comments more personal and meaningful to all of us who heard her.

The general themes of discussion covered topics on zero tolerance (regarding violence), childcare, community involvement, hotlines and better school climate. Secretary Richard Riley addressed the need of lower class size and providing better supervision of children at home and school. The main federal focus, though, was on reducing the number of guns and not on stopping attacks.

Mrs. Sarah Brady spoke for her husband, James Brady, who was a victim of gun violence when he was shot by John Hinckley Jr. in March 1981 during Hinckley's assassination attempt on President Reagan. The president was hit in the chest and James Brady was hit in the head. The attack left Brady brain-damaged and unable to speak. The attack turned Brady into America's best-known crusader for gun control. After the shooting Mrs. Brady became chairperson of a gun control group called Handgun Control and Center to Prevent Handgun Violence.

President Clinton made a promise at the last conference to analyze the recent school shootings, determine what they had in common, and what steps could be taken to reduce the chance of similar tragedies.

Clinton said, "We do not understand what drives children to pick up guns and take the lives of others. We may never make sense of the senseless, but we have to try."

To summarize the federal response, it failed to focus on prevention. We weren't asked for our input on what could stop attacks or how to spend money on interventions like Korem's and doing best practice studies.

The result was an undated FBI study released in 1999, *The School Shooter: A Threat Assessment Perspective*. It concluded there wasn't a profile of the shooter and provided little of value to prevent attacks other than to form assessment teams and encourage students to come forward if they hear about an attack.

Following Columbine, the Secret Service and the Department of Education released its May 2000 report which concluded there isn't a profile of the school attacker, and no guidance on where these incidents would and wouldn't occur and why. Like the FBI's report, the best advice given to administrators like me was to encourage our students to come forward and report an attack if they encountered anything suspicious. But we were already doing that.

After Columbine, we received student threats. So I called our students to the auditorium and decided to do something unusual. I explained to them that the irresponsible actions of just a few students were taking their school hostage. I challenged them to do something about it and come forward with information and to encourage others not to do something foolish. That day, the threats stopped. But I don't advocate that administrators should *depend* upon teenagers when lives are at stake. As we know, kids can be excellent observers, but not always the best interpreters. Most of the schools that used the 3-point intervention we've discussed didn't have detailed discussions with students about reporting suspicious behavior, yet their threats stopped. It's appropriate to ask students to help, but not to take the lead.

Overall, the federal response was frustrating. The FBI knew that Columbine was supposed to be a bombing attack. How would gun control have stopped those bombs from going off?

After the White House Conferences, we returned to our respective school districts and formulated our own programs of recovery and prevention. We promoted character education in the elementary grades, conflict resolution and peer mediation training in grades 6-12, and mentor programs for the lower grades. We attempted to secure federal and state help for security personnel mainly through grants. Statewide we solicited help from the Veterans Administration, the Governor's office and the Department of Education. Many secondary schools added police to their staff. Some were former police hired by the school district instead of relying on the regular city or county law officers. Several thousand were trained by Dan Korem. Attacks were averted in Plano, Texas, the resort town of Gulf Shores, Alabama, and Glenbard, a suburb of Chicago, among others.

At Pearl High School we did add police to our staff, which has continued today. That idea came from our community planning sessions after our press conferences following our incident. It provided assurance for parents that they could send their children back to school. Nationally the "student resource officer," as they are called in most schools, provide positive intervention before crimes are ever committed. It was made clear by our parents and community leaders, however, that severe armed fortification of our campus was inappropriate and not the right response.

Another positive initiative we started was an anti-bullying program. It struck at the heart of what happened at Pearl High School. As you read my thoughts and research on the bullying factor, please remember that if you bully students who *don't* have the Random Actor profile, it is unlikely they will commit an attack. But, if you bully students who *do* have the profile, there is an increased risk of an attack.

Bullying often causes its victims to suffer depression and other stress disorders and illness, as well as loss of self-esteem and relationship problems. All that is reason enough to stop bullying wherever it rears its ugly head. But when the victim's profile includes a combustible mixture of Random Actor attributes, the result may also be an explosion into Random Actor rage.

Therefore, creating a zero-tolerance attitude toward bullying is beneficial for all students and is the right thing to do when backed up by appropriate responses. Because of the connection between bullying and some cases of Random Actor violence prevention, I will spend some time sharing thoughts from my research on the subject of bullying as it affects the entire student body. Also, we will look at Korem's Missing Protector Strategy, which he developed in the late 1980s and reduces most at-risk behavior and will benefit almost any at-risk student.

Bullying

A successful playwright told me about how she was a victim of bullying on her very first day of school in her Mississippi hometown. As she entered a side door, two boys attacked her, scattered her belongings, and hit her repeatedly. She went directly to the principal and asked for help. The principal took the emotionally upset child by the hand and went to each room looking for the bullies. Once located, the boys were suspended and reprimanded by the principal, who made it clear that there would be no bullying in her school. This is the best outcome, but in some schools it would not happen.

How serious should we take the bullying issue in our schools? The extreme effect of bullying in the Pearl attack put bullying on every educator's radar. By 2009, the American Academy of Pediatrics recommended for the first time that schools adopt a prevention model developed by Dan Olweus, a research professor of psychology at the University of Bergen, Norway. The model he says works at the school, classroom, and individual level and combines preventative programs and directly addresses children who are involved or identified as bullies or victims or both.

"Dr. Rober Sege, chief of ambulatory pediatrics at Boston Medical Center and a lead author of the new policy statement, says the Olweus approach focuses attention on the largest group of children, the bystanders. 'Olweus's genius,' he said, 'is that he manages to turn the school situation around so the other kids realize that the bully is someone who has a problem managing his or her behavior, and the victim is someone they can protect.'"[1]

"By definition, bullying involves repetition; a [student] is repeatedly the target of taunts or physical attacks—or, in the case of so-called indirect bullying (more common in girls), rumors and social exclusion. For a successful anti-bullying program, the school needs to survey the [students] and find out the details—where it happens, when it happens. Structural changes can address those vulnerable places—the out-of-sight corner of the playground, the entrance hallway at dismissal time."[2]

Stege says that "activating the bystanders" means changing the culture of the school; through class discussions, parent meetings and consistent responses to every incident, the school must put out the message that bullying will not be tolerated."[4]

In light of the statistically significant number of Random Actor youths in schools, policy backed by thoughtful action that discourages bullying is prudent; it reduces their irrational behavior and the possibility of one youth destructively directing another.

Students learn at an early age the importance of liking and disliking their peers. We adults can still remember how devastating it was to lose favor with a friend and, in the case of a bullying victim, to lose a whole school and feel completely alone.

Bully traits first appear in grades K-3 but are well defined in the 6-8 grade middle school setting. The male bullying behavior is usually aggressive and negative, often carried out repeatedly. There is usually a relationship demonstrating an imbalance of power between the parties. Experts believe bullying happens to both sexes equally according to Child Psychologist Kenneth Wessel. With girls, however, the behavioral pattern is different, with the victim often forced into social isolation through indirect antagonism. Girls try teasing, spreading gossip, criticizing the victim's manner of dress and other socially significant markers including race, religion or disability. Derogatory remarks about a person's family, especially one's mother, one's home, personal appearance, or sexual orientation are effective and stir resentment, fear and anger.

According to the National Resource Center for Safe Schools, 30 percent of American children regularly are involved in bullying either as bullies or victims. Approximately 15 percent of children are severely traumatized as a result of encounters with bullies. Researchers conclude that bullies soon after or before leaving school become engaged in criminal activity including heavy drug use. Those who are bullied develop anxieties, depression and are often dependent upon the taxpayers to treat their illnesses.

Daniel Goleman in an article written in *The New York Times* calls the bully a paranoid, lifelong loser. Goleman quotes Dr. Leonard Eron, a psychologist at the University of Illinois at Chicago, in a 22-year study, 1960–1982, that provides valuable insight involving 870 children, approximately half from each sex, tracked from the time they were 8 to 30. The following is the common bully life cycle outlined:

Age 8: **Schoolyard aggression**—starts fights over nothing
Friendship—often social outcast
Difficulties at home—parents view as hard to control
Intelligence—falls within a wide range
Academic performance—scores below potential
School life—dislikes school and expresses defiance

Age 19: **School**—likely to have dropped out
Criminality—three times more likely to have trouble with the law
Friends—viewed as trouble maker by peers
Intellectual Skills—performs below innate potential on achievement tests.

Age 30: **Marriage**—spouse views as aggressive, abusive, too quick to anger
Work—often in a job requiring skills, native ability
Legal Troubles—run-ins with the law, drunken driving, crimes of violence
Fatherhood—like parents, uncaring and punitive, children tend to repeat the pattern, son is a bully

Overall, bullying occurs when someone keeps doing or saying things to have power over another person. Bullies tend to fight, intimidate, kick, hit, bite, or act in an aggressive manner with often-destructive consequences. Bullies see threats that do not exist and always feels that *their* anger is justified. Bullying is possibly the most underrated discipline offense that occurs in any school setting.

Evidence that I gathered from Luke's teachers, especially in the early grades, was that he was happy and exhibited characteristics of a normal childhood. He was a good reader and above average in his learning skills. His mother attended PTA meeting and showed supportive interest in her son. After completing his work, Luke often volunteered to help other children who may have been having problems.

We know that this positive trend did not continue. Luke's problems first came at home after his father divorced his mother and left the home. Next, his physical features of being overweight with poor eyesight combined with a low self-esteem fueled by his mother, who blamed him for her divorce, blended into a victim profile that gave the school bullies something to target.

When he became old enough to seek the attention of girls he was rejected on more than one attempt for friendship. These rejections increased his low self-esteem.

Next the fate of every mother's concern that their child is running with the wrong crowd became a reality. The old saying fits that, "no friends are better than the wrong friends." Luke was targeted by Boyette, a college student who graduated from Pearl High School the year before. Boyette was a popular boy from a well-respected family but he had a dark side. This connection was not what Luke needed. Boyette fed off Luke's low self-esteem to become his mentor, and led him in the wrong direction.

A person becomes a bully usually as a way of being popular, or of making himself look tough. Some bully to get attention or to make others afraid of them. They may also be jealous of the person they are bullying. At home they may have been bullied themselves.

This brings us to the question, "Is a bully born?"

If they are treated harshly at home bullying may be an attempt to regain self-esteem by acting aggressively toward others or trying out what they have learned. There is much evidence to conclude that bullying is often a family problem where parents teach them to strike back if confronted. Often there is too much freedom at home and lack of supervision. One thing is for sure; bullies need victims and they waste no time in seeking them out.

The victim is physically weaker, often overprotected at home and withdrawn from the activities of the other children. The victim is just different in some way. It can be the color of his skin, the way he talks, his size or just his name. In most cases, victims look as if they won't stand up for themselves. If they become frightened or insecure they may resort to use of weapons to protect themselves.

Not all school settings are like the one that Luke faced, but for many students the number of similar occurrences is more numerous than educators would want to believe.

Bullies seek out areas where there is minimal adult supervision. Common areas of conflict are in locker rooms, hallways, playgrounds, restrooms, and on buses where drivers focus most of their attention on the road. Bus confrontations have always taken a high percentage of administrator's time as drivers generally are not trained to handle discipline problems. Some help in this area comes with the aid of cameras on buses and volunteer supervisors on the buses. Some rules can help such as assigned seats with the known problem students seated at the front of the bus. Suspensions from bus privileges after a set number of infractions can get the point across to offenders.

Today, a new trend has emerged: electronic or digital bullying. Using text messages, email, distributing photos, etc. is now commonplace in schools. It also makes it easier for students who don't have the physical presence to bully, to become bullies and hide behind their digital facade. It is also common for even sixth- and seventh-grade students to threaten suicide. It's a school counselor's nightmare.

Regardless of how it presents itself, persistent bullying may have a number of effects on an individual and in the environment where the action takes place. Among those effects are depression, post-traumatic stress disorder, anxiety, aches, pains, and gastric problems —as well as loss of self-esteem and relationship problems.

Effects of bullying upon a child's character can be long lasting if not corrected. Sometimes damage can be reversed but many times the loss of self-esteem lasts a lifetime. Ron Stephens, the former director of the National School Safety Center, says that bully victims whom he interviewed told him they could still remember the name of the bully who had tormented them in grade school fifty years earlier and the details of the confrontation.

In Iowa in 1993, Curtis Taylor, an eighth-grade middle school student, committed suicide to end his torment after three years of bullying. He withstood name-calling, being bashed into a locker, chocolate milk poured down his sweatshirt, and vandalism of his belongings. Testimony indicated that the school administration repeatedly failed to intervene. To the extreme, some experts call this "bullycide." In my opinion, bullying has similarities to rape in that the offense is often under-reported because of the humiliation and the self-directed disclosure connected with the lawsuits and the ensuing media coverage.

Since the increase in school shootings and the proliferation of media coverage, juries are now more likely to sympathize with the victims, and many victims have sued bullies directly for intentional infliction of emotional distress. Also, parents have sued schools, teachers or administrators who failed to adequately supervise the student's activities during the school day.

Common sense dictates tells us that interventions are not always successful in the same way for each child. I have found that multiple attempts to find the right one are often needed. One form of mediation, for example, is for the bully victim's parents or caregivers to invite the bully and his legal guardians to a conference at their house. Parents and children can discuss what should happen in the future instead of assigning blame for the reason that the meeting was originally called.

Giving a child karate lessons is sometimes helpful if he has been victimized. It demonstrates support from the parents and encourages self-esteem on the part of the child.

My two grandsons ages 9 and 10 were bullied by older boys on their regular school bus route. After seeking help from the bus driver and the school principal, which was not successful, my daughter took the boys off the bus route and organized a weekly auto shuttle system with other parents who were having similar problems. This way the parents did not have to transport the kids more than once or twice a week. It wasn't the best solution, but the kids were happy with the arrangement. This option would not work, of course, for working parents. This approach, though, does nothing to correct a bully's behavior; any real solution must affect both the bully and the victim.

Building a peer group for the targeted student may be another approach. A student should be told if a bully has a weapon; striking back is not the answer. A young child should scream for an adult, try to wiggle out of the bully's grasp, and run. The best intervention is when a school staff of teachers, counselors, and administrators have set the rules of conflict and do not allow exceptions. Administrators should never allow teachers to promote common myths—such as that victims are responsible for bringing bullying on themselves, bullying is just a normal part of childhood, bullies will stop if you just ignore them, or bullying will only stop when victims learn to stand up for themselves.

When parents think their child has been bullied, they should have a conference with teachers and/or administrators to gather the facts before taking action. Often, all the facts have not reached the parents through the student. The administrator after a conference can put out an alert if there is a need.

In most cases responsible school authorities can find a solution. If, however, the problem persists, the parents should act on their own by going to the superintendent, school board, or the police for help. If this doesn't work home schooling or private school or legal intervention remains as last resort options. Ultimately the last stand in protecting children rests with the parents or caregivers. They should under no circumstances allow their child to be bullied continually without making an effort to solve the problem.

When I was in high school, I was over six feet tall, over two hundred pounds, and the captain of my school football team. I didn't experience the feeling of being a bully victim while growing up. Vicariously, however, through my two daughters, my grandchildren's experiences, and forty-plus years in education have made this a personal concern.

My youngest daughter, Susan, suffered with low self-esteem, possibly from our moving from one school setting to another when she was young. Each move brought an entirely new group of classmates all at one time. Yet, she surprised her entire band membership when she challenged a bully band member to an off-campus showdown to settle their differences. I don't know who got the best of the showdown, but I know bullies never bothered her after that time.

As my daughter matured I noticed an increase in her self-esteem, which brings me to believe that input from teachers, parents, and role-models make a difference. She and her husband are college graduates working in full-time foreign missionary service. Many times students can solve their own problems by deciding to stand up for themselves, but usually they need help.

Schools have a responsibility to establish rules of conduct involving bullying with proper suspensions or expulsions. Each class should have codes of conduct similar to the following: no hitting, punching or kicking, no name-calling or put-downs, everyone is included in group activities and we all help others when they are being bullied. Every effort should be made to protect victims of physical or mental abuse while they are in school.

The reasons for school shootings are multifaceted. However, I consider bullying to be at the heart of student conflict. I feel that to take advantage of a person just because you are stronger is to say you have no respect for another human being, do not honor the laws and rules of established order, or have either empathy or an appreciation for fairness and justice. We recognize that bullying is not confined to individuals in the school setting. Research tells us that groups of people have been victimized by others in their environment throughout history. The Native American Indians depicted by the historical period in the 1830s called the "Trail of Tears" were forced off their land in the Southeastern United States to sanctuaries west of the Mississippi River to get them out of the way for land development by the people in power at the time.

My great-grandfather William W. Dodson migrated to the "Trail of Tears" Cherokee Indian Territory called Tallequah in northeast Oklahoma in the late 1800s before its statehood. His son, my grandfather, Will H. Dodson, returned to Mississippi, where he married my grandmother and raised his family and told us stories of the Indian mistreatment from his experiences. From his accounts and my research, I have concluded that the bullying treatment by the U.S. Federal Government was for real.

While living in the Mississippi Delta and after serving as an administrator in that region at Greenville High School, I witnessed the mistreatment of African-Americans whose ancestors had been slaves. I was involved with the Civil Rights movement where folks were trying to right the sub-human conditions that began during slavery. I saw the resentment and distress on their faces as they protested the second-class citizenship during the integration era to defend the right to vote, run for office, use public facilities, and attend the public schools.

I've traveled to Munich, Germany, and to Auschwitz, Poland, in 2002. (*Auschwitz* is the German rendering of the Polish town Oswiecim.) I witnessed first-hand at the museums and memorials dedicated to the Jewish people and others who were involved in genocide of their people during the Second World War. Oskar Schindler's actions, well documented in the book and movie, *Schindler's List*, show how those who care can stand up against the bullies of tyranny. These examples of international bullying and inhumanity made me even more convinced that the seed of bullying should never be allowed in our schools.

As we saw in Pearl, but on a smaller scale, bullying had the same facets as these historical maladies. We have problems with both the bully and the victim of bullying. The bully may become involved with criminal activities while the bully victim may cause both death and destruction.

We may fall short of our goal to match the accomplishments of Oskar Schindler and Martin Luther King in making a difference for human kind but we must believe that collectively we can be successful. It will take all of us including caring parents and an informed community to reach our goals. Much suffering has taken place from the tragedies at Pearl, Paducah, Jonesboro, Columbine, and Virginia Tech, let alone the less the lesser incidents that didn't get this type of publicity. It is incumbent upon all of us to help bully-proof our schools.

One direct way that we can protect not only victims but bullies, too, is through the Missing Protector Strategy (MPS).

Missing Protector Strategy

From the late '80s to the mid-'90s, Dan Korem tried to solve the riddle of why youths joined gangs from low-crime suburbs and small towns—educated and affluent communities. He found that globally youths who joined gangs had one of the following six risk factors.

- Divorce
- Separation
- Physical abuse
- Sexual abuse
- A severely dysfunctional parent
- Both parents working full-time jobs, but both don't have to work full-time jobs

Added to the above are students where the parents have never married, which now accounts for about half of all U.S. births.

Obviously many students have these risk factors but don't join gangs. What Dan wanted to know was: *Is there something else that when added to the at-risk home makes a student vulnerable to gang recruitment?* Dan found that tipping point: the Missing Protector Factor. He developed a strategy to provide students with "protectors."

The Missing Protector Strategy was used in Dallas County (1986–1992) with more than 400 inner-city youths, and the results were profound. One-third of the youths had seen somebody shot, stabbed, or murdered. The majority of the students were African-American (75 percent), Hispanic (20 percent), and the rest Asian or Caucasian. The results were out of proportion to the effort expended in the high-crime, gang-infested neighborhood. Not one youth joined a gang, not one girl became pregnant, and classroom performance for most immediately rebounded. What follows is adapted from both *Rage of the Random Actor* and *Suburban Gangs*.

Missing Protector Strategy Research

Numerous studies have demonstrated that if a youth doesn't feel safe and protected, classroom performance deteriorates—a common sense connection. In 1992, while in Budapest, Hungary, speaking at various universities, Dan Korem was introduced to the seminal research of Dr. Maria Kopp, a psychiatrist and sociologist at Semmelweiss Medical University. Dr. Kopp is both a researcher and practitioner at a family clinic. At the time, Hungary had the highest suicide rate in the world for teenagers—16 percent. Nearly 1 in 6 had attempted suicide in 1988; the U.S. rate was half, 8 percent. For the last fifteen years, Hungary has had one of the highest suicide rates per capita for all age groups.

In her co-authored study of over 21,000 Hungarians, she found that the lack of a Protector when faced with a crisis was the number one factor that drove teen suicide. She also found a one-to-one correlation between those who didn't have a Protector and gang involvement and chronic drug use. Korem published portions of her research in *Suburban Gangs*. Here are some of the study's important findings with observations in parentheses.

- Of the 1,555 youths (ages 16–20) surveyed, 22 percent expressed that they couldn't count on an immediate family member or extended relative or friend in a crisis. This virtually coincided with the same 21 percent who experienced some form of depression, neurosis, expressing itself through suicide, drug use, gang and cultic involvement, criminal acts.

- Youths who can count on a parent during a crisis are more likely to have future life goals, complain less of anxiety and melancholy, are less likely to attempt suicide and have less hostility to the environment, consume significantly less alcohol and commit fewer crimes.

- Frequency of criminal convictions for a youth is almost solely tied to the [family protector factor].

- Poor financial conditions by themselves do not typically cause clinical neurosis or depression.

- After the age of 20, a youth does not seem to be as

vulnerable to the Missing Protector Factor, probably because a youth becomes more independent. (I would also add: 1. youthful hormonal change also begins to level. 2. one now has more mobility and the ability to get away from or find distractions for what is troubling.)

- The statistical breakdown of those who experienced depression in the Hungarian population related to the status of their family was as follows:
  — Married and spouses living together (5.5 percent)
  — Divorced but spouses live together because of financial considerations (13.5 percent)
  — Divorced and spouses not living together (14.6 percent)
  — Separated and not living together (16.8 percent)[5]

After the release of *Suburban Gangs*, educators and law enforcement called for prevention assistance related to the burgeoning gang trend. Over time, a refined application of the Missing Protector Strategy developed as briefly described below:

What a Protector does—A Protector is an adult who lives in the neighborhood and whom youths can call for assistance if faced with a crisis. A crisis can be anything from a friend trying to induce them to use drugs, failing several tests, parent leaves the home, a divorce, girlfriend or sister gets pregnant, etc. A Protector is a unique type of mentor whose sole focus is protection. Other types of mentors, for example, may meet with a youth several times a week for reading lessons, go on outings, be a "significant other" who befriends them, etc.; but a mentor may or may not be a Protector who lives in the neighborhood and responds if a youth is faced with a crisis. The two most important attributes of a Protector is the ability to communicate with a child and the commitment to respond when there is a call for help. The Protector's primary responsibility is to help a youth faced with a crisis.

Protector responsibilities:

1. Agree to be a Protector for at least two years.
2. Meet with the student every other week.
3. Telephone the student once a week as a "check-in" call.
4. Respond to a call for assistance if a youth is faced with a crisis. Protectors for the most part are neighbors who can relate to kids. A Protector is not expected to be able to solve every problem a youth might face, but like a caring parent, "they show up" and try to help. (A list of professionals is provided to Protectors whom they are directed to call for assistance when presented with a severe situation—school counselor, juvenile officer, youth pastor, etc.)

Who initiates the Missing Protector Strategy—The strategy is usually initiated by schools as they have the greatest access to children, but local churches and service organizations often become part of the volunteer process as well. When organized by a school or school system, the usual background checks and policy considerations are followed accordingly, like the screening and direction given to other school volunteers. In a school setting, Protectors are selected and screened by administrative staff, counselors, parent-teacher leaders, etc. Because the time commitment is small, most schools can quickly recruit Protectors, unlike most excellent mentoring programs that require substantial time commitment.

Methods for identifying students who need a Protector and matching with a Protector:

1. Anyone who knows a student who needs a Protector can inform the school (or other organization).
2. The method that reaches the greatest number of students is to present the idea of the MPS directly to students in

student presentations. It is explained that most students who get involved in high risk behavior often don't have a Protector. It is expressly stated: *If you don't have someone you can call night or day if you are faced with a crisis, let someone here know—a teacher, your principal . . . and they will find someone for you.* Volunteer Protectors attend the school presentations, and their presence has a powerful impact on students. They see that people do care and will help. Approximately 2–5 percent of the students in a typical non-inner-city school will request a Protector. Matching students with a suitable adult of the same sex is facilitated by designated staff or other trained professional. MPS presentations are useful from grades 3 through 12.

The diversity of communities that have used the MPS demonstrated that it can work in any community:

Inner-City Community (Dallas, Texas, 1986–1992)—Previously cited.

Affluent Suburb (Plano, Texas, 1998–2005)—A community that persistently experienced many high at-risk youth trends since the 1980s, including teen suicide and over 18 heroin deaths (in one period of eighteen months). Since 1998, over 1,000 at-risk students have received Protectors and less than 10 percent have displayed at-risk behavior in a specific year, including student who had a "hit list" but never carried out attack after receiving a Protector.

Culturally Diverse Hispanic Community (Odessa, Texas, 1999–2002)—Applied in a program targeting students not fluent in English who were truant. A dramatic drop in truancy followed.

Small Rural Town (Blum, Texas, 1999–2002)–School district with approximately 300 students. Five youths received Protectors. After two years, one of the youths had a severe at-risk episode.

Canadian Community (Chatham, Ontario, Canada 2001–2004) Following the tragic death of a 10-year-old elementary school youth, this community of 100,000, 60 miles northeast of Detroit, launched the MPS. Within 90 days, 30 youths were matched with Protectors. An independent 6-month preliminary study of the results of the initial application of the MPS in the Chatham-Kent, Ontario community, found results consistent with other communities, including:

- None of the children demonstrated any at-risk behavior while they were with their Protectors.

- One interesting finding was the fact that none of the Protectors had to respond to a crisis call from their assigned [at-risk] child. This is especially important as the MPS is centered on the premise that Protectors be available in times of crisis.

- Protectors saw positive changes in the child's academics (improved grades, better attendance), peer relationships (positive connections with peers), overall behaviour (happier, better understanding of right from wrong, increased self-confidence, a decrease in fighting, better problem solving skills) and their involvement within the community (structured community activities).[6]

————•————

To reemphasize, students with the Random Actor traits should receive *both* the 3-point intervention and a Protector as required. The Protector concept can also be applied in any organizational setting for an adult with the Random Actor traits. An on-the-job Protector, for example, might be a team leader who mentors a staff person in professional areas of expertise.

CHAPTER 12

OTHER ISSUES

———•———

In this short chapter, I will briefly comment on specific trends that are likely to affect the Random Actor school attack issue for a number of years, some of which are from Dan Korem's ongoing research.

Bringing guns on campus

A misguided movement is gaining momentum to allow students and staff to carry concealed handguns on campus. In April 2009, on the anniversary of the Columbine attack, three professors, including two from the University of Texas at Dallas (UTD), wrote a nationally distributed Op-Ed in which they presented their case why people with concealed-handgun permits should be allowed to carry their weapons on campus. The professors were Theodore Day, finance professor, Stan Liebowitz, economics professor, and Craig Pirrong, finance professor at the University of Houston.

UTD is located in Richardson, a statistically safe Dallas suburb that is the headquarters for Texas Instruments, which helped establish the campus to provide staff for its company. UTD is a part of the University of Texas System and has several excellent schools including business and engineering.

Here is what the professors wrote in their Op-Ed entitled, "Put guns on campus:"

Mass public shootings are a horrific feature of modern life. Many of the bloodiest examples of this scourge have occurred on college campuses. As professors, we are particularly sensitive to this danger.

Despite this — no, *because* of this — we support a bill currently pending in the Texas Legislature that would permit the concealed carrying of firearms on college and university campuses by holders of concealed-handgun permits. . . .
Mass public shootings occur almost exclusively in places — like universities — where concealed carry is proscribed [prohibited]. . . .

Gun-free zones are magnets for killers bent on maximizing their body count. They know that they face far less risk of quickly being stopped there.

First, they do not understand the correlation that these shootings almost always occur on campus environments, like Pearl, that are statistically safe and represent the Manager quadrant to killers. The fact that these communities are statistically safe is one reason that gun-free zones are established, and people don't feel a need to carry a weapon.

I am not opposed to some handguns being on campus that are in the possession of a law enforcement officer or someone like our Joel Myrick, who was in the National Guard and grabbed his gun from his truck and used it to help apprehend Luke. But to allow anyone who has a permit to carry a gun on campus is misguided and is not supported by most school law enforcement professionals. Purely from a tactical perspective, its difficult for the untrained to successfully shoot at assailant and it would be a nightmare for law enforcement arriving on a scene to determine who is and isn't the shooter.

As demonstrated by Korem's research, many Random Actor

school killers *were not* on anyone's behavioral or law enforcement radar. To allow anyone with a permit to legally carry a weapon on campus would make it more likely for a Random Actor with a permit to act on impulse and kill someone.

Additionally, carrying guns on campuses will not stop a bombing attack, as was intended at Columbine or at DeAnza College (25,000 students) in January 2001 in San Jose, California, a suburb of Cupertino.

Ironically, in 2002, Korem called 35 of the highest-risk U.S. colleges and universities that most represented the Manager quadrant and warned officials that they were at risk for an attack and told them why. UTD was one of those campuses, where two of the professors are currently employed. At the time, a significant number of students where threatening homicidal-suicidal acts. No action was taken. Then, after the 2007 Virginia Tech attack, a UTD human resources official attended a Random Actor violence prevention training at William and Mary College and recommended the deployment of the intervention strategies.

Several meetings with senior UTD officials ensued. All except a new campus executive wanted to deploy the strategies. He blocked the rest of the officials; the strategies were never deployed. A staff behavioral expert, the chief of police, were vocally displeased when deployment was blocked. As a courtesy, Korem explained that based upon his survey of the campus, the highest risk "Manager" target on the campus for an attack was the engineering school.

On January 9, 2009, John Shaffer, a 20-year-old computer science major with the Random Actor profile, randomly selected a female engineering student in an engineering building and stabbed her in the neck. Two weeks later, a Virginia Tech economics student *beheaded* another student in the student café—another unprecedented attack.

Guns would not have stopped either Random Actor attack, but understanding how to identify the Random Actor traits and the 3-point intervention might have. To date, neither campus has deployed the Random Actor prevention strategies, even though senior officials at both campuses recommended it.

As long as campuses do not prevent attacks that are preventable and tolerate the large number of daily threats that disrupt campuses and put campuses at risk, there will be more calls for carrying guns on campus for protection.

The new "hoaxes" that *must* be investigated

Until a year or two ago, if Korem was asked for a law enforcement consultation when a threatening inscription—a graffiti-threat such as "the school will pay on October 12" for example—was found in a bathroom, on chalk board, etc., he advised, based upon experience, that it probably wasn't a real threat. He found that most Random Actor killers with intent usually didn't want the world to know they were going to attack. They wanted the element of surprise.

Unfortunately, that has changed.

Case after case is now surfacing where students wrote threats or placed hoax devices to make people afraid, and *then* planned an attack. Such a case is pending, for example, in Virginia Beach, Virginia, where a student created a "hoax" device and two years later was found in 2009 with explosives and an alleged plot to take out the school. At the same time in a Dallas suburb a student who made bomb threats in 2007 was caught with what was characterized as a "serious plot." It seems that because threats and evacuations are now common place, these students are seeking attention and want to be taken seriously.

If this trend continues, as is expected, this means that without forensic evidence or the ability to identify if a student has the Random Actor profile, it will be very difficult to accurately assess intent behind a hoax. This means a severe drain on education and law enforcement resources and time to investigate, assess, evacuate, and so on. On the other hand, such threats can be a warning, a herald of future intent—and therefore identifies some who should be watched and "defused."

Standardized testing and the Random Actor threat

It may have just been a coincidence that Luke launched his attack on the first day of standardized testing in Pearl. He alleges that it was the day Boyette said to launch the attack. If so, Boyette was in college and wouldn't be affected by what was happening on campus, but Luke may have been affected.

Standardized testing and the way it is usually facilitated represents the severe actions of the Manager quadrant—in the box, no change, inflexibility, control, etc.. Administrators are increasingly finding authentic Random Actor threats during this type of testing and the preparation instruction leading up to the testing day. As noted in Chapter 8, Random Actor attacks usually hit McDonalds but not Jack-in-the-Box which is *outside the box*. Similarly, it isn't wise to convert a campus to a *check-in-the box* environment when you are trying to reduce the temperature to prevent an attack.

The administrator in Chapter 9 who highlighted in his evaluation that the teachers were under "extreme pressure," tells us that they were paying attention to the task of test taking and not the students, as evidenced by sustained Random Actor threats on his campus. To his credit, he allowed his principals to receive Random Actor violence prevention training, but wouldn't allow his teachers to receive even an hour's overview. He was afraid that this would put too much on the teachers' shoulders, when actually it would have been a release valve that would have *decreased* tension. His reaction is common, but providing some change, variability, and flexibility is needed to reduce the potential of an attack or threat. Precisely how this is done should be left to each campus, but administrators must allow and empower staff to apply these themes as required.

If you're a parent, consider this email from a teacher to her family. Her building was evacuated during a standardized test preparation day. Then, ask yourself, *is this what I want for my child's school?*

I just wanted to let you all know today went really well. Every student was searched, patted, and wanded as they entered the doors. We had roughly 1,000 students absent today (the most kids I had in a class was 11, and I usually have 26-30). . . . Thanks for your prayers today!

Spiritual Divide

Anyone would agree that when students are murdered by the hands of other students, we are compelled to examine beliefs, values, and the lessons we teach. Perhaps something is missing; perhaps something should be done differently. Although the reasons behind such serious behavior are admittedly multiple and complex, the spiritual void in the lives of these young killers usually surfaces, as it did for Luke Woodham.

As earlier noted, Korem uncovered in his research that approximately 70–80 percent of Random Actors who kill, spiritualize their rage. They don't just kill; they seem compelled to inject a spiritual twist with anthems like:

Push this button, slay the heathen, and you will enter Paradise

Call me God

I killed my family so I knew they would enter heaven

Follow me and you will not succumb to the Apocalypse[1]

This certainly fit Luke Woodham. Bullied, isolated, from a broken home, he thought God deserted him and joined a satanic gang. It was his Random Actor slam against the Church, which represented the Manager traits: the Conventional Ten Commandments and those with a Confident faith in God.

As Korem pieced together case after case, he found it wasn't uncommon to see irrational spiritual twists for Random Actors who kill. They use the spiritual to artificially prop up their paranoia and justify crazed acts.

Saddam Hussein, for example, had pints of blood drawn from his body and then directed scribes to create a special "martyr's edition" copy of the Koran using his blood for ink, as shown here. Each of the 6,000 verses and 336,000 words were penned using his body fluid. He then individually displayed all 640 pages in a specially constructed Mother of All Battles mosque, built in Baghdad to commemorate his "victorious" invasions of

Kuwait in 1990—all this even though it's considered blasphemous to Muslims to use blood to inscribe a copy of the Koran.[2] There are many other equally bizarre examples that most of us have never

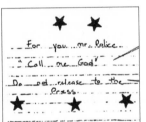

heard about.

Lee Malvo, the teenage sniper of the Muhammad-Malvo duo who killed at least 10 and wounded 13, on October 22, 2002, left authorities a note at one of the crime scenes in which he wrote, "*Call me God*," and demanded $10 million dollars in cash.

In 1933, Adolph Hitler, was Germany's new Chancellor. He created the National Reich Church and had an entire copy of the Bible rendered with all references to Jews removed. He did so in a crazed attempt to martial the forty-five million Protestant Germans. It created a political firestorm and was front-page news around the world (right, from the November 30,

Whole Nazi Church Cabinet Resigns in Dispute Over Bible

Bishop Mueller to Appoint New Group.

'KEEP GOSPEL'

Assures U. S. Reich Will Stand by Testament.

BERLIN, Nov. 29.—(AP)—The whole Reich church cabinet, governing body of all Protestant groups in Germany, resigned tonight in a crashing climax to the bitter church controversy over strict adherence to the letter of the Bible.

The resignations, including that of Bishop Joaquin Hossenfelder, who withdrew from his official position yesterday under pressure from the cabinet, were accepted by Reichsbishop Lodwig Mueller.

Picking New Cabinet

Chicago Hostess Heroine as Plane Falls in Icy Lake

Stands Neck-Deep in Water to Supervise Rescue of Nine Passengers.

WINDSOR, Ont., Nov. 29.—(AP)—Climbing from the submerged cabin of a large airplane which crashed in Lake St. Clair, nine passengers and a crew of three sat on top of the wings of the ship until rescuers broke their way through ice and brought them safely ashore tonight.

The plane, an American Airways craft, piloted by Dean Smith of Summit, N. J., was forced down by engine trouble.

Landing was made on the thin sheet of ice covering the lake, near Peche Island, close to the Canadian shore.

WINGS HOLD UP PLANE.

The body of the plane crashed through the ice, but the wings prevented it from going to the bottom in some thirty feet of water.

1933, *Chicago Herald and Examiner*).

And finally, Mohammed Atta, the 33-year-old lead attacker on 9/11, became an extremist only after his father, an affluent Cairo attorney who was also a Random Actor, divorced Atta's mother after 40 years of marriage. Atta, who was never religious before the dissolution of his parents' vows, then became a religious extremist and killed people of all faiths, including Muslims, when he flew a hijacked American Airlines passenger jet into the north tower of the World Trade Center.

That Luke Woodham later recanted his satanic obsession and embraced Christianity speaks to a severe spiritual divide that existed in his life; one that might have been bridged and prevented the attack. Two inmates reached out to him and provided spiritual protection— for him it was both immediate and eternal. What if another student or caring adult had touched that need before the attack?

In the summer of 1998, another young man in a small east Texas town, whom we will call Russ, plotted a shooting attack on his school. Like Luke, he was bullied, from a broken home, new to his community, and had no protector. In a lengthy taped interview, he explained to Dan Korem his torment and why the attack never happened. Here is an excerpt from that interview.[3]

Russ: I didn't walk right. I didn't talk right. There was something about me that wasn't appealing to the other students. I was persecuted by a lot of people. That's what I felt. I came in and I was desperately looking for friends, and I picked the lowest people to hang out with because they were the easiest ones to be accepted by. I don't want to say that some are lower than others, but I did hang with those of a lower social status. . . . When you get to school, you wish you were back in [the town where I grew up]. You get picked on a lot and you're afraid to do anything about it. Everyone fights together and you're the only one you have. Your mother can't be with you. I got tormented and picked on all the time.

DK: Now you say "torment" and not "taunt."

Russ: The bullies or whatever you want to call them liked to mess with others and torment others. That's what you're going through. People might mess with you and stuff and taunt you, but when they back you into a corner, they're not trying to taunt you, they're pushing you back and bearing down on you. And, that's the way it was.

DK: When did you realize you were really getting ticked off and that you might want to hurt someone?

Russ: I cried myself to sleep most nights. One morning I woke up and I thought to myself: I don't hate myself. I hate everyone else. There's nothing I've done to deserve being treated this way, so I might as well start doing it back. And I was still a coward. I could fight if someone came to my home. That's your territory. But you don't know what is going to happen when you're somewhere else. . . when I was in the 6th grade I got my first [hunting] rifle and I was a lot braver hiding behind the barrel of a gun.

Then Russ describes what happened that prevented the attack. The elderly gentleman in the church had no idea that Russ was plotting a massacre.

Russ: I was walking to [a friend's house to get the last gun] and I passed by a church and the parking lot was full. When I was six, I used to go to church, but when I hit the fifth grade I quit. So I wanted to see what was going on in there, so I snuck into the back row and sat down next to an old man. I don't remember anything about the sermon, but it was just this old man and me on the row. At the end of the service, he reached over and hugged me. He embraced me. Told me how he was so glad that I came and how much he was looking forward to seeing me next Sunday. He asked me my name, where I was from, the names of my parents, and how I was doing. I just didn't know what to think, but I liked it. It was love and I knew it, and I hadn't felt that forever. It was something I had almost forgotten about it. It was a real love, and I came back the next Sunday for it—and the next Sunday, and the next Sunday. And I was asked to check out the youth group. And the people were nuts—they were having a good time. They weren't mean to me. They didn't cuss at me or ask me for money. They just took me in like I was one of theirs. It was something positive, and I started weighing these things out. The way I was acting when I was at church and what was going on at school and what I was doing and running around with my friends doing bad things and the things I was planning to do. I just looked at them [circumstances in his life and his reaction to them] and I decided that I liked love better. I liked being a part of something, which is something I always wanted. And it was great.

When there is a school attack, students globally pray and look for spiritual comfort and answers to mortal and eternal questions.

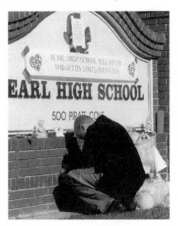

It's what our student, Adam Scott, did as captured by a local news photographer, J. D. Schwalm . . . as students do all over the globe after an attack.

When young lives are cut short because of a car accident, disease, or violence, we all look for answers and comfort. This is expecially true when the life of a young person ends because of a crazed act.

After another Random Actor massacre on March 11, 2009, in the statistically safe town of Winnenen, Germany, students did the same as our students. They prayed and sought spiritual solace from each other, family, and teachers.

We allow and encourage prayer and expressions of faith when tragedy strikes. We don't discourage students in desperate need to seek spiritual solace and direction. I have come to the conclusion that schools also shouldn't prevent students from similarly expressing their faith through prayer or other forms of expression *before* they are

Students spiritually reaching out in faith after Tim Kretschmer, 17, killed 15 students, teachers, and others in the German town of Winnenden, dwarfing the death toll at Columbine. It was Germany's second worst massacre in a country that has some of the strictest gun laws in the world. The words "Wir trauern um eush . . ." translate, "We are mourning for you . . . "The word "Warum" translates, "Why?"

faced with dark days. This uncoerced expression of faith is not only helpful to students who are just navigating day-to-day decisions, but it can also prevent an attack. The elderly man at church didn't know anything about Random Actor behavior when he reached out to Russ, yet he unwittingly stopped an attack through the thoughtful expression of his faith.

I am not advocating state-mandated religious instruction and prayer, rather tolerance for the appropriate expression of one's faith as it relates to the school environment and the mentoring and nurturing of students. Rachel's Challenge is one such program that touches students. It was started by the father of Rachel Scott, one of the victims at Columbine, and doesn't advocate a specific faith or

dogma. It has been presented to millions of students with an almost
universal positive reception by both students and educators. The roots
of the presentation come from a haunting spiritual place as revealed
in the book, *Rachel's Tears*. Months in advance of her death, Rachel
wrote in her personal journal about the anguish and depth of despair
she witnessed in many of her classmates. Here is the first verse of a
poem Rachel wrote before she was murdered.

> People are crying.
> Losing their minds.
> People are dying,
> Taking their lives.
> Will anyone save them?
> Will anyone help?
> Will somebody listen,
> Or am I all by myself?
>
> Please reach out your hand,
> Grab a hold of their life.
> Open their eyes,
> To His wonderful light.
> Let them know,
> Of His undying love.
> That this comes only,
> From Heaven Above.
>
> Please reach out your hand,
> Grab a hold of their life.
> Don't let go,
> Without a good fight.
> Witness to them,
> Show them the way.
> Give them God's love,
> And give it today.
>
> I sit here and tell you,
> To go save a life.
> But what am I doing
> To give that good fight?
> I judge other souls,
> Never checking my own.
> Oh my Lord,
> I should have known.

People are crying,
Losing their minds
People are dying,
Taking their lives.
Will anyone save them?
Will anyone help?
Will somebody listen,
Or am I all by myself?

I don't have all the answers, but my experience at Pearl sugests
that both we and our young will profit if we find ways to bridge the
spiritual divide in our personal lives.

CHAPTER 13

THE UNLIKELY JUROR

DR. CHRISTINA DANIELS

———◆———

This is Dr. Christina Daniels' account of her experience as a juror. I met her for the first time at an educational workshop I led. By accident I discovered that she was a juror at the second Luke Woodham's second trial in Hattiesburg, Mississippi. Her juror account is unique and reminds us of the process that unfolds when we *don't* prepare to prevent.

In May of 1998, not long after I started a new job with a local non-profit organization, I came home to find my husband, Eddie, laughing at me while holding a jury summons. Until that time, I had only been summoned to jury duty twice. He, however, seemed to have been on the "Most Favored Juror" list for our county. I grabbed the envelope out of his hand and threw it on the kitchen counter and began to fix supper. Somewhere between the hamburger and the helper, I opened the summons and spread the paperwork on the counter.

There was something unusual about this particular jury summons. The envelope was heavy and I saw some instructions that were unfamiliar to me. I looked at Eddie and said, "It's a sequestered jury . . . they want me to pack a suitcase."

We discussed the summons and then I dismissed the notion of being selected. At that point, it had not occurred to me that this was a summons for the Woodham trial. All previous summons Eddie and I had received had been for petit jury duty. This one was different. I folded the paperwork and stuffed it back into the envelope. I gave the envelope to my foster daughter Misty and asked her to take it and put it in my car so that I could give it to my employer. As Eddie, Misty, Harvey and I sat down to eat supper, thoughts of jury duty quickly gave way to other family issues and I soon forgot all about it.

The next day, I took the jury summons to work and gave it to my boss. I was a bit apprehensive about telling her I might be out of the office for a week. I had just started a new job and feared that a week-long absence might not be welcomed with open arms by my supervisor. She sat down in my office, read the summons, and said "No problem. Do what you need to do."

As I discussed the summons with her, I suddenly realized that this could be a summons for jury duty for THE trial. I heard on the local news that the trial of Luke Woodham was to be held in Hattiesburg. The dates matched up and it was logical to assume that the jury in that trial would have to be sequestered. I asked myself aloud, "Why hadn't I seen this before?"

On the night before I was to report for jury duty, Eddie and I discussed the possibility of my being selected and being away from home for an extended period. The previous October, we had become guardians to two teenagers, and Eddie was suddenly faced with the prospect of having to be Mr. Mom.

On Tuesday, June 9, I reported to the Forest County Courthouse for jury duty. I had not packed a suitcase because as I believed I was probably not a stellar candidate for jury duty in this particular trial for a number of reasons. I had a Ph.D. in Education with an emphasis in criminal justice. I was a certified teacher. I had worked as a teacher for the Mississippi Department of corrections. My brother,

Ken, worked as a K-9 officer for the Department of Corrections. Eddie's mother Martha, his dad Kenny, and three members of my extended family were all certified public school teachers. I had no reason in the world, whatsoever, to think that I would be given a seat on that jury.

As I entered the courthouse lobby, it was apparent that this would be an extraordinary trial. I walked through the metal detector and my purse was searched by a deputy, which was unusual in 1998 for most trials. Entering the rear of the courthouse, I took a seat near the back.

As I clutched my juror information card, I looked at a woman who was sitting to my right. She seemed anxious, so I asked her if this was her first time to be summoned for jury duty. She said, "No," but expressed reservations about being selected. She told me that she owned her own business and she was the only employee. She told me that having to shut her business down for a week would be financially devastating for her. I told her not to worry . . . that in past instances, an employer letter was usually instrumental in exempting Eddie and me from jury duty. I told her that I could think of no reason that the judge wouldn't send her home.

At the time of the trial, the Forrest County Circuit Judge was Dickie McKenzie. He was always in great demand as a speaker at local events because of his incredible sense of humor. I looked around to see if he was in the courthouse and mentioned to the lady to my right that, at least, we would probably be entertained. To my surprise, a distinguished unfamiliar man, Honorable Samac Richardson of Rankin County, took the judge's chair.

Preliminary introductions of the judge, the bailiff, and the court reporter and the prosecution and defense teams were followed by some harsh words by Judge Richardson. He told prospective jurors that the court had been inundated with requests to be excused from jury duty after the first round of potential jurors were summoned.

He told us that a second round of summons had to be sent out to ensure an adequate pool of candidates for jury duty. He then told us that no one in the room should assume that they would be excused if a request was made.

As he began questioning jurors who petitioned to be excused, I leaned over to my neighbor and told her "I have a baaad feeling about this."

She leaned over and said, "Me, too."

When she was called to approach Judge Richardson with her request to be excused, I watched but could not hear their conversation. She returned to her seat next to me. With teary eyes, she said, "He said No."

After the last juror who requested to be excused had been heard, Judge Richardson told us that we would now move into the portion of the jury selection process known as voir dire. Voir dire, a legal phrase derived from the French Language, means "to speak the truth." Both the prosecution and the defense can examine juror responses on the juror questionnaires and ask each juror questions to determine whether or not they should be excluded. Each side is allowed a specific number of peremptory challenges-opportunities to excuse jurors if there is a bias against either side in the trial.

I relaxed a bit. I thought that as soon as Woodham's attorney found out that I was a teacher with a criminal justice background I would be sent home. To my surprise and disappointment, the only question Mr. Roussel, Woodham's attorney, asked us that related to teaching was whether or not any of us were members of a teacher's union. I could not truthfully say that I was a member of any teacher's union. Although I was certified to teach, I had not by that time, joined any professional teaching organizations or unions. As the questions continued, my heart began to sink.

After all peremptory and for cause challenges had been made and accepted by Judge Richardson, I looked around and noticed that the crowd had thinned out considerably. As both the prosecution and defense conferred to make final juror selections, I began to feel nauseated. Judge Richardson told us that as our juror numbers were called out, we were to stand, walk over to the jury box, and take a seat. He told us that fifteen of us would be selected as jurors—twelve jurors and three alternates. He said the alternates would not be named until immediately prior to deliberations, as he wanted all fifteen of us to listen to the evidence with the assumption that we would have to decide Woodham's guilt or innocence. As my eyes scanned the courtroom, I began to figure probabilities in my head.

With each juror selected, my level of anxiety increased. As juror 14's number was called, I thought to myself "just one more." The last number called sounded familiar to me . . . it was the one on the card I was tightly clasping in my right hand. I was juror 15.

As I took a seat in the jury box, I looked at the man to my left and asked him, "Did you pack a bag?"

"No," he said. "Did you?"

I shook my head and said, "What are we gonna do?"

After the courtroom was cleared of everyone who had not been selected for jury duty, I asked one of the deputies in the courtroom if I could call home. As juror after juror confessed to the judge that they had not brought clothes and personal items, he made arrangements for us all to call home and have family members drop off our things in the lobby of the hotel at which we would be staying. I don't remember exactly what I said to Eddie when he answered the phone, but I told him that I needed him to bring me some clothes and personal items to the lobby of the local Cabot Lodge. He didn't handle the news well, and I realized that my experiences as juror 15 were going to be difficult.

Sheriff Billy McGee stopped me in the lobby of the hotel and told me that Eddie had brought my things and had become angry with him because he was not allowed to see or speak to me. Patience is not (and has never been) one of Eddie's virtues. As Sheriff McGee stood there explaining "the rules" to me, I apologized and told him that I had neglected to bring a suitcase because I had assumed that, based on my personal and professional experiences, I would have been sent home. I explained that we recently became foster parents for the first time and that some of Eddie's reaction was probably his frustration and fear of taking on unfamiliar parental responsibilities. After all was forgiven, I took my bag and settled into my hotel room for the night.

We were all housed in the same wing of the hotel. Law enforcement officers were stationed inside the building to provide security. Because we would probably be exposed to trial-related publicity, television channels that might report trial coverage were removed from our televisions. This didn't present a problem, until we realized that we wouldn't be able to watch the NCAA Basketball Playoffs. A few of the jurors complained to Sheriff McGee and he told us he would see what he could do.

On the first day of the trial, we were transported to a local Cracker Barrel restaurant for breakfast. As we sat and ate as a group, I noticed restaurant employees peering at us from the kitchen. Before we left, the waitress who was in charge of our table asked us all to sign a copy of our ticket so she could have our autographs. I turned to the man behind me and said, "Did she just say what I think she said?" He nodded, and I shook my head and walked out to the van.

As we approached the courthouse, the deputy driving our van told us that we were to enter the courthouse quickly and not speak to any reporters. When our van came to a stop, one of the jurors said "Oh, my God! It's CNN!" Positioned all around the courthouse were news station satellite trucks representing stations and networks from around the United States. It was, literally, a media circus. It was also the beginning of what seemed like the longest week of my life.

After Judge Richardson briefed us, we waited in a jury room until he was ready for us to take our seats in the courtroom. We were each provided a small legal pad and writing instruments. He told us that any notes we took regarding the testimony we heard had to be recorded on our pads. He also said that, under no circumstances, were we to discuss anything at all about the trial prior to deliberations.

As I waited for the trial to begin, I looked around the packed courtroom. All around us were Pearl High School students, family members and friends of the victims, and some local residents who had showed up early to snag one of the few vacant seats left in the room. After the preliminaries were out of the way, Judge Richardson asked the deputies assigned to the trial to escort Luke Woodham into the courtroom. As we waited for him to enter, the courtroom crowd became silent and everyone's eyes were on the rear door of the courtroom.

In spite of having seen pictures of Woodham in media coverage prior to the trial, I was taken by surprise when he walked into the room. I was expecting to see a monster. After all, a normal person couldn't just walk into a school and kill children. A monster could. I was surprised and, quite honestly, disappointed to see that Luke Woodham was not a monster. He was, in my opinion, quite plain. He had no distinguishing features; he was, in fact, pitiful and unremarkable. As he sat down, I saw him push his glasses up onto the bridge of his nose with his finger. He blinked his eyes and looked around the room. At that moment, he reminded me of a frightened little boy on his first day of school. I supposed that "anticlimactic" is the only way I know how to describe the way I felt when I saw Luke Woodham for the first time.

When we returned to the hotel after the first day of the trial, we were told that arrangements were made with the hotel to provide an opportunity for us to watch the basketball playoffs. I walked to my room and changed into some comfortable clothes. We were allowed to make monitored phone calls on a limited basis. I called home and

Misty answered the phone.

When I asked to speak to Eddie, she said "WHEN are you coming home?" I was relieved to know that all was well at home. I told Eddie that they were predicting the trial to last until Friday. I told him that I was OK, and that I missed him.

After hanging up, I weighed my options for the remainder of the evening: watch basketball with a bunch of people I didn't know, watch whatever happened to be on the Lifetime Movie Network, or take a shower and go to bed. Although I'm not a basketball fan, the prospect of watching the game was a whole lot less depressing than sitting alone in a hotel room with no one to talk to. I walked downstairs to an odd sight.

The hotel had cordoned off a small lobby with a large screen television in it. A Forrest County Deputy was in the room and was required to get up and turn the television off each and every time the station went to a commercial break. Judge Richardson had insisted on this order to shield us from any media coverage of the trial. I remember thinking that the Deputy would probably be more exhausted than the basketball players by the time the game was finally over.

Early Wednesday morning, we were again taken out for breakfast before reporting for duty. As we later rode to the courthouse, a couple jurors said that they thought we were being followed by reporters. By the time the trial was over, the courtroom had become a sanctuary for me . . . no reporters in hot pursuit and no reminders of the fact that I was, at least in my mind, so far away from my family.

As I listened to the testimony throughout the trial, I tried desperately to sort out the facts of the case in my mind. Mr. Woodham's defense team never disputed the fact that he was responsible for the murders of two classmates and the aggravated assaults of seven others. They even acknowledged the fact that Luke had just been convicted of the murder of his mother Mary Woodham during a trial in Philadelphia,

Mississippi. School administrators, teachers, students and mental health experts all testified about the events of October 1, 1997.

During the trial, the facts revealed that Luke drove to school after stabbing and bludgeoning his mother to death in their home. At around eight o'clock, the regular opening time for school, He walked into a common gathering area at Pearl High School with a rifle that he made no attempt to conceal. There, he shot Christina Menefee, a sixteen-year-old girl he had briefly dated. She died from a rifle wound to the chest. Also killed was Lydia Dew, another classmate. By the time he fled the scene, two girls were dead and seven other classmates were wounded.

During the melee, Assistant Principal Joel Myrick ran out to his vehicle and retrieved a handgun he told the jury he used for personal protection. Myrick pursued Luke as he left the scene. When Luke wrecked his mother's car, Myrick detained him with his gun until authorities could arrive and assist him. I distinctly remember hearing Myrick recount the words Luke said to him as he stared down the barrel of Myrick's pistol.

He expressed surprise that Myrick did not know his name, and told him "I'm the guy who gave you a discount on your pizza." I remember thinking to myself, "What kind of person opens fire in a public school one minute, and then talks about pizza discounts the next?"

In opening statements and as the facts in the case unfolded, Woodham's defense team maintained that it was their belief that he was not responsible for his actions because he was legally insane—something they called a "Defect of Reason." Specifically, they claimed that his actions were the result of an emotional hold that members of a cult-like group called the "Kroth" had over him at the time of his crimes.

The Kroth, the defense argued, was a group of teenagers who had regular meetings to discuss grandiose plans to wreak havoc on those who wronged them and escape to Cuba to live happily ever after. The self-proclaimed leader of this group was a young man named Grant Boyette. Boyette presented himself to Woodham as a philosopher and satanist who was capable of casting spells. He appealed to Woodham's loneliness and lack of a sense of belonging. I remember Woodham describing a turning point in his relationship with Boyette. Woodham stated that Boyette had allegedly "cast a spell" on a young man who had reportedly been picking on Luke.

According to statements made by Woodham, the object of Boyette's spell was struck by a car and killed a short time after the spell was cast. Woodham eagerly accepted these circumstances as "proof" that Boyette was, in fact, empowered by Satan. According to Woodham, it was Boyette's voice that urged him to murder his mother on the morning of October 1, telling him that he was "spineless" or "gutless" if he didn't take revenge on Christina Menefee for breaking up with him.

Eight years of post-secondary criminal justice training prepared me to sort out the information provided to me in the trial, to look at graphic evidence photos through the eyes of a problem-solver instead of a curiosity-seeker, and to make an educated decision based on the facts presented and the law. It did not, however, prepare me to read the twisted journal entries of a young man who gleefully described torturing and killing a family pet.

I remember when Luke's journal entry detailing the brutal torture and killing of his dog was introduced into evidence. He described how he and other members of the Kroth squirted a flammable liquid into the dog's throat and burned her "inside and out." As the other jury members and I heard graphic testimony about the contents of Woodham's journal, I glanced over to see a couple of jury members show signs of becoming physically ill as a result of what we were hearing.

The journal writing expressed joy over the dog's suffering and exhilaration over the sense of power gained from completing a "first kill." Throughout the course of the trial, memories of that testimony constantly flooded my thoughts.

When I returned to the hotel after that testimony, I called home to check on my family. Although I couldn't share with Eddie any details of the trial, before I hung up, I began to cry and asked him about our dog, Bebe. He reassured me that she was fine, and that he and the kids were watching over her.

"Why are you so worried about the dog?" he asked.

I wanted and needed to tell him that I missed them all . . . even the dog. I told him that I loved him, hung up the phone, and prayed that the trial would be over soon.

Woodham's defense presented expert testimony asserting that he was legally insane at the time of the shootings. There is no doubt in my mind that Luke felt unaccepted by his peers at school. I also believe that he was bullied and mistreated by some of his classmates. As the defense worked diligently to persuade us that Woodham was not responsible for his actions because of the fact that he was so emotionally wrecked by years of abuse heaped on him by his family and then by his classmates, I struggled with the question "At what point and to what extent is it OK for someone to fight back?"

As Friday drew to an end, Judge Richardson asked the jury if we wanted to continue to deliberate or whether we wanted to recess for the evening. We sent back word that we wanted to continue to work toward a verdict. At this time it was certain to all that the decision was imminent. When the jury reappeared in the courtroom, the consensus of those in the courtroom was that the verdict would be to convict. Our jury chairperson stood and informed Judge Richardson that we had found Woodham guilty of all charges against him. She had tears in her eyes. She wasn't the only one.

After the verdicts were read, Judge Richardson immediately sentenced Luke to life in prison for the murder of Christina Menefee, life in prison for the murder of Lydia Dew, and 20 years for each of the seven aggravated assault convictions. After sentencing, Woodham stood and offered an apology. He told the Court that if he had been sentenced to die he would have deserved it.

The mother of one of the murdered girls stood and told Woodham that he was the reason she would never be able to hold her grandchildren. He was then led away in handcuffs.

Barring some unforeseen miracle for him, he will die in prison. I looked at the members of the jury and felt satisfied with our decision.

Judge Richardson sent word to the jurors that because the trial ended late in the day that we could stay in the hotel for an additional night and our families could join us for a relaxing evening. When we got to the hotel lobby, many of the jurors made phone calls to family members and asked them to come to the hotel to spend the night. I leaned over and told the deputy that I wanted to go home. I missed Eddie, Misty and Harvey, and my dog. I really, really missed my dog. I climbed into the front seat of a patrol car and never looked back. I was so thankful that the trial was over and that I would soon be able to see my family. It was my first ride in a patrol car and, for some reason, my thoughts turned to Luke Woodham. I wondered how things looked from the back seat of the patrol car in which he was riding. I felt sad . . . for his victims, their families and for him.

After the trial, I met Leslie Roussel, Woodham's lead defense counsel and members of the prosecution team. When Mr. Roussel spoke with me about my impressions of the trial, I told him that I was still shocked to have been selected and why. I told him that I was surprised that he didn't ask more probing questions during voir dire. I think he seemed a bit surprised by what I told him.

I often think about what this experience has taught me and how I have used what I learned as a juror. Hopefully I have used my knowledge to keep other potential Luke Woodhams from doing what he did. But, I still like working and championing the causes of the underdog.

I have found myself somewhat overprotective of children who were, in my opinion, the victims of bullying. I have tried to spot potential victims and perpetrators early on and become very proactive at heading off problems before they start.

I have often been asked the question, "What is your most memorable experience in education?"

My answer often surprises many people. In 2003, my first year in Picayune Schools I was named Teacher of the Year. In 2004, I was named a Congressional District Finalist for Mississippi Teacher of the Year. In 2005 I received the Mississippi Teacher of the Year Award and *USA Today* named me to their All Teacher Team. These teaching honors have afforded me professional experiences that, unfortunately, many teachers never enjoy during their careers. I have spoken to civic groups, published articles in national journals, and even received a hug from a President of the United States while standing in the Oval Office at the White House. Today, however, if I'm asked about which experience stands out in my mind and has been most instrumental in helping me to become the educator I am today, I would have to respond by simply saying, "jury duty."

CHAPTER 14

HEROES

I define heroes as people admired for their bravery, great deeds, or noble qualities. George Washington for me was a hero who provided leadership to fight for our country's independence and then tackling the job of becoming our first president.

Other heroes may be less significant in the world's eyes, but their heroic contribution is found in the eye of the beholder. A child's mother or father usually fits this category. Hopefully his teachers would qualify as well.

After our attack, my heroes or heroines were the students, faculty and administrators who endured the hardships of facing the nightmarish reality of our tragedy.

I admire them for overcoming their innocence, but most of all for their determination to face a school, community, and personal tragedy that affected each of us.

Chelsey Kelly, our homecoming queen and a class officer, best summed up our thoughts when she was interviewed by Dan Rather of *CBS*.

She told him that no one student much less Luke Woodham had the power to take away the excellent qualities of her school and of her high school classmates. An African-American and selected for distinction by her peers, she showed the nation something special.

During the weeks after the attack, we experienced a string of student successes; awards and victories in band, choral music and athletics seemed to prove what Chelsey conveyed. Our band members marched in the Macy's Thanksgiving Day Parade in New York City a few weeks later. All the TV networks interviewed the "Pirate" band officers and helped them to keep their spirits high.

To conclude this short book, I've asked students and staff to share their thoughts with you. These teens, are now adults, who look back with hindsight on a day that shook their world. They and those who guided them at Pearl will long be my heroes and heroines.

A TALE OF TWO CITIES
Chelsey Kelly

"It was the best of times. It was the worst of times."

Charles Dickens' opening line from *A Tale of Two Cities* is an excellent description of my senior year. The memories of my senior year bring me happiness as well as sadness.

The good times were numerous, but the bad times were more profound. A fellow student went on a shooting rampage at my school and two people were killed. When I recollect the shooting, my heart frowns. Tears come to my eyes when I recall the destruction of the reputation of my school and the city that I love.

Because their children suffered, the Pearl community, as a whole, suffered and had to begin coming together to heal its wounds. Teachers, students, school administrators, parents, pastors, and city officials all built stronger relationships determined to overcome the tragedy that changed Pearl forever.

The staff of *CBS 48 Hours* interviewed me extensively, perhaps, because they had staff present at our homecoming game when I was crowned homecoming queen. Although the excitement of being interviewed by Dan Rather was overwhelming, it was somewhat tempered when reality set in and I was forced to face the real reason he was in town.

As time passed, incidents similar to the one that occurred in Pearl took place elsewhere. My school reached out to help others that had reached out to help us earlier. The Pearl community learned by our incident that we were not immune to violence that we previously thought was occurring elsewhere in the world. The present focus on youth cannot bring back the lives already lost. It hopefully can prevent further harm.

WERE YOU THERE?
Tara Yeager

On October l, 1997, I was getting ready for school. I packed up my books and headed out the door. The only thought in my mind was finding one of the cute guys I had discovered since I started school.

After arriving at school, we heard a crazy noise. It sounded like a firecracker. In the commons early in the morning, everything echoes. The only thought in my mind was that someone was about to get in a lot of trouble for setting a firecracker off at school.

Still clueless and curious, I came out from behind a trophy case where I had gone after the first shots. I was blessed since a friend had pulled me out of the range of fire. At that point, everyone ran for cover. I could see a boy in a black trench coat behind us with a rifle. I dropped my book bag and lost one of my shoes.

Soon there were police cars and ambulances flying into the parking lot. Now outside, I remember feeling the car shake as the police cars rushed by. There were parents at the entrance to the parking lot wanting to know if their children were okay. News reporters were everywhere. I can honestly say that I could live a full and happy life without seeing another reporter again. I cannot begin to describe how stressful and annoying it was to have a camera shoved in your face after the incident was over. There were reporters calling my house, cameramen everywhere. At that point, our little town and school needed some peace, not more chaos.

It wasn't until much later that I realized that those first two shots took the lives of two innocent girls. Two girls who were best friends, two girls whose parents had sent them off to school fully expecting them to return home at the end of the day. A person should never have to be afraid to come to school.

I wonder why every time we have a bomb threat or even a loud noise, I shake uncontrollably. Waves of panic go through my body. I hope all the bad stuff is over and it will never happen here again or anywhere else. Yet, as long as there is evil in this world, I have my doubts. A lot of people say it's just life. That may be true, but sometimes I wish life didn't hurt so badly.

THE DAY I WAS SHOT
Robbie Harris

School violence in Pearl was a non-issue except for the occasional fight. I thought it was constrained to inner-city schools and usually based on drugs or gang activity. I learned the costly lesson that this was not true. People anywhere can have enough hate in their heart to seriously injure and slay other human beings.

Then came the sound that has made one of the biggest impacts on the lives of so many citizens of Pearl. I remember thinking that the sound was a cannon the school had been using to celebrate touchdowns. Was the whole thing a senior's joke? Then came the motion. Everyone was moving. As I picked my foot up, I felt a pain shoot through my leg. The working of the muscles caused me to lose so much blood that I left footprints down the hall as I ran.

The trial the next summer was one in which I testified. Seeing Luke for the first time was sort of eerie. I had never seen him at the high school. Some of the ones that had been hurt wanted him to die. Why do we want to take another life? If the world is full of nothing but vengeance and hatred, this plague will never end.

TIME STOOD STILL
Corey Rogers

That morning I walked through the wet grass on the band practice field; I talked and joked with my friends as I did to start a normal day. When we were about halfway across the field, people started running out every door in the school. I remember thinking that it looked like the battle scene in *Braveheart* where there was just a solid wall of people running.

Someone yelled, "There's a guy with a gun in the commons shooting people!"

I remember thinking how the people looked like cattle, all of them running as fast as they could, following whoever was in front of the crowd, running over each other.

My dad finally got to the band hall and took me from the school. When we got to the entrance of Pirate Cove, reporters were blocking the road. They were like sharks, sensing blood and each wanting a piece of the action. The sight of them and all the stories afterward gave me an entirely new prospective on the news media.

THE EXPERIENCE
Erica Mason

On October 1, 1997, I saw the sign of Pirate Cove for the last time through the eyes of an innocent child. The sign would not change that day, I would. A policeman stopped our car and told the driver to turn our car around, someone had been shot.

I was at a new school with new people, about to experience life. No one thought two classmates would be murdered. No one entertained the thought of a tormented boy walking into our school with a gun. I was not worried about murder, death, or losing someone I cared about. Those thoughts belonged in the adult world. The event changed my life. My major priorities in life have become family, loved ones, school and myself. The most important thing that the shooting taught me is life can change within seconds. Luke Woodham not only took someone's life, but he also robbed many of his or her childhood. Death is one of the hardest things to endure; yet the students at Pearl High School had to adjust without a lifetime of experience.

REFLECTIONS OF THAT DAY
Brandon Willis

The events of October 1, 1997, will forever remain etched in the walls of my mind. I will always be able to hear the shots and see the terror in the eyes of my fellow classmates and teachers. A student who decided to take his unhappiness and frustration out on innocent victims victimized us.

As we rode around to the front of the school, a shocking sight appeared in front of us. As we got to the front of the school, I saw Mr. Myrick running across the grass wielding a handgun. I soon realized that he was making an attempt to stop the shooter. Mr. Myrick ran towards the car. The car ran into one of the small trees planted at the entrance to the student parking lot. My emotional state was one of sheer terror.

As a multitude of police vehicles kept pouring in, news reporters also began to approach the school rapidly. Reporters got out in a frenzy and began interviewing anyone in sight. I was interviewed four times within a short period.

We watched the news later and learned that the gunman's name was Luke Woodham. Who is Luke Woodham? Why would he want to do this to his school, our school? What could fill someone with such rage and hatred that he could kill his own mother and classmates? How could this blatant act of hatred solve any problems that he ever had? What did this prove except that he is one of the most ignorant human beings that ever walked the face of the earth?

I never thought anything could have such a profound impact on our entire community until I saw and experienced first hand such a horrific and terrible thing. It did, however, bring the community closer. I found myself hugging people I didn't even know at memorials.

CONFUSION IN THE MORNING
Drew Mitchell

What's happening? These were the only words that came from my mouth as I found myself running among my terrified peers. I heard people say something about a gun. It was not until that answer was given that I knew why I was running. Robbie passed me, and I looked down and saw his foot. It was saturated with blood. There was a trail of red footprints where we had traveled.

My dad is the pastor of First Baptist Church in Pearl and is also chaplain for the Pearl Police Department. He went with the police to the school. He told me how he had seen my book bag sitting motionless amid bullet shells and how his heart sank. He quickly set out to find me. He traced me to my friend's house and embraced me tighter than anyone has ever done before. Tears flowed from his eyes as he told me how glad he was to see me.

I'm not usually one to be disturbed by much, but I promise that I heard a shot when I awoke the next morning that made me sit straight up in my bed. I breathed heavily when I realized that the terror was over.

I had no idea about the shadows that lurked behind the atrocity—cults, conspiracies, and plots of mass murder plagued the news. Through the course of one week, a normal school was transformed from a place of education to a temple of fear.

The aftermath of the tragedy caused students to embrace one another with love. Friends formed among enemies. Companionship flowed through us that had never been seen before. Every time there is a reoccurrence elsewhere, the wounds are reopened.

We have learned to hold the hands of God. He points us to the direction we must travel, and that direction is forward. Looking back only halts the progress. I have learned how easily life can be destroyed. We must never take what we have for granted because it can be ripped to shreds at any moment. We must have faith that God is in control, and that is something nobody with or without a gun can take away.

THEY DIED IN MY ARMS
Charles Sandler

My military training earlier in my life did not adequately prepare me for what happened at my school on October 1, 1997. I was a naval science instructor at Pearl High School where I had worked for eleven years.

The shots rang out loud and clear: Bang! Bang! Bang! What I saw was someone holding a hunting rifle in the commons where students gather prior to the beginning of classes.

I looked down and saw Christina Menefee, 16, one of my students, lying on the floor in a pool of blood. She had been shot in the neck. I tried to stop the bleeding, but I was unsuccessful. Christina died in my arms. A few feet away Lydia Dew, 17, was dying of a bullet in her back. I cradled her in my arms, telling her that she would be all right, but she, too, died of her wounds.

I later learned that the shooter was Luke Woodham, a 16-year-old sophomore at the high school who had also killed his mother, Mary Ann Woodham, with a knife earlier in the day.

EYEWITNESS ACCOUNT
Becky Rowan

This day began as any other day for me, a high school counselor at Pearl High School. I remember being anxious—not because I anticipated the unimaginable event that transpired, but because of statewide testing for approximately 300 ninth graders that would be set in process partly under my responsibility.

As I walked across the commons, a large, open area where students gather before school, a few students were already there at 7:30 a.m. when I arrived. Lydia Dew always stood or sat close to the door of my office. I remember on that morning, like many others, we spoke to each other. Lydia was very excited that day because class rings were going to be delivered and she wanted to know what time the representatives would be there.

At approximately five minutes after eight, I was standing at the door of my office talking with a friend. We heard a pop, which sounded like a firecracker. My friend and I started toward the door. As I heard the second pop, someone screamed, "It's a gun!"

Soon everyone was running for cover.

In the room in the counselor's complex, another teacher said it was Luke Woodham. She had actually seen him shoot. He was a student of hers. It was hard for me to believe that the shooter was our student.

We walked out of the counselor's office after we were told the shooter had gone. I saw several bodies on the floor. Book bags were everywhere. It was deathly quiet. Then, along with several other teachers, I tried to help the wounded and dying. The first student I got to was Lydia Dew lying on the floor by my office door where I had spoken to her earlier. We talked to her, not realizing how seriously wounded she was, and told her that she would be okay and that help was on the way.

I left Lydia with two teachers and walked over to Christina Menefee, Luke's former girlfriend, whom he had shot at point-blank range with a hunting rifle. Two teachers were there trying to stop the bleeding, but it was hopeless. I remember that her hands and her face were already blue. I walked to Alan Westbrook, who, as he tried to run from Luke, was shot in the back as he grabbed a girl to shield her from the bullets.

One of the most vivid memories of that day was Lydia's mother arriving at the scene. I did not know until after I was outside the building that Lydia had died. I remember Joel Myrick, our assistant principal, who had subdued Luke, walking with Lydia's mother across the lawn. Big tears were streaming down Joel's face, as he knew what news was about to be shared with this mother. Joel, the big, husky, military guy. The guy you would think would be the last person you would see afraid or crying. My heart broke. I realized that this nightmare was not a dream. It was real.

GRADUATION
Shelley Boudreaux

One sunny, unsuspecting Wednesday morning little did we know our lives would be changed forever. Even though the media discussed nothing but negative aspects of the tragedy at our school, we were blessed with stronger friendships and increased faith. Our faith has grown stronger. This faith has guided us through the year and will continue to carry us into our future.

The class of 1998 will not focus on the negative

The class of 1998 should be remembered for our achievements

The class of 1998 is a class of hope

Some of my heroes still live in the area. Others are as far away as the states of Washington and California. I have been able to contact most of them and updated their activities, both those in this chapter and others introduced in other chapters.

Chelsey Kelly, our homecoming queen, is now a nurse at a local hospital. She is married to a successful optometrist and is the mother of a one-year-old son. She is more aware of other people's feelings and tries to interact where there is suffering.

Robbie Harris, who was wounded by Luke, graduated from the University of Mississippi with a major in Business and later from Georgia Tech in Engineering. He now works for Honeywell in Harbor City, a suburb of Los Angles. He married a Pearl girl and is trying to settle into his new job. His faith is a major part of his life; the attack moved him closer to God. He has forgiven Luke for shooting him and credits the tragedy with giving him guiding insight for life.

Corey Rogers, the son of a church deacon and ex-school board member, has graduated from the University of Mississippi majoring in International Studies. Single, he is in his second year of law school at the University of Washington in Seattle.

Drew Mitchell, the pastor's son who watched his dad work closely with the school to provide counseling after the incident, has graduated from Southern Mississippi University in Hattiesburg with a major in advertising and marketing. He and his wife live on the Mississippi coast in Gautier where she teaches math at the local high school. He works for a local ship building industry. He says the tragedy caused him to be more sensitive to others around him, and he will never take safety for granted ever again.

Commander Charles Sandler since retired from the school system. He cradled both girls in his arms before they died. He wanted to help but it was too late. I have visited him since his retirement watching him engage in his favorite activity. He and his wife work regular volunteer shifts at a local hospital helping the sick and those in need of medical attention. He seems happiest when he is helping others.

Our counselor, Becky Rowan, continues to love her church and plays the organ at each Sunday service. She still works as a counselor at Pearl and provides care for our students.

Shelley Boudreaux Langley, the class salutatorian, who wrote and read a positive poem about her class at her graduation is now married and after graduating from the University of Southern Mississippi is now employed as a nurse. She lives and works in Brandon, Mississippi and is employed by Camellia Home Care. I asked Shelley what lessons in life she may have learned from the tragedy. She said she was not in the Commons at the time of the shooting but said because of that she felt a guardian angel must have kept her away. Because of her senior year's involvement in the tragedy and its aftermath she will never take life for granted ever again.

Roy Balentine, the young principal who had only been on the job as a principal for four months prior to October 1, is now in private business.

Joel Myrick, our assistant principal who stopped Luke's assault, is still a school administrator. After leaving Pearl High, he served as a principal in Gulfport, Corinth, and now Hancock County in Kiln, Mississippi. In 1999, Joel was presented the Soldier of Fortune Humanitarian Award in Las Vegas, Nevada, for his feat of heroism. In the eyes of the former students, teachers, and administrators who witnessed this school disaster we collectively feel he was our hero.

I wasn't able to contact Tara Yeager, Erica Mason, or Brandon Willis. When I do and have their update, I will post them on the "Live Addendum" page for this book provided by International Focus Press (www.ifpinc.com) on its website.

I'm not a poet, so I don't have a verse to bring this book to a close. But for years, I was an educator and a professional who oversaw the education of tens of thousands of children and teens. Today, I am busy giving lectures on what I have learned on my journey as well as what happened on that day that changed all of our lives.

I hope you have learned something from what we experienced, and that you will put into action the violence prevention strategies discussed in this book and that they will prevent this type of tragedy in your community.

We've had more than a decade to make sense of that awful day—to recover. Recovery is something one has to do oneself, however. There are different ways to regain normalcy in your life. In the case of the students, teachers, parents and citizens of the Pearl Community, it came slowly and painfully but the perseverance of those who believed in themselves managed to lead the rest of us back to a proud community filled with hope for the future.

ACKNOWLEDGEMENTS

I extend heartfelt thanks to those who helped make this book a reality:

Publicist Barbara Travis, whose efforts in my behalf resulted in my publishing in major magazines and who encouraged me to write this book. Terry Giroux, Gary Reed, and Kay Baker, whose collective efforts created the spark that lit the fire. Tim Hickey, whose proposal found Dan Korem and the International Focus Press. Dan Korem, who became not only my publisher, but my friend and confidant. My editors, Paula and Paul LaRocque, for their masterful editorial skills. Susan Leigh and Sue Mary Holiday—for their editorial contributions and faith in the project. Joel Myrick and Dr. Christie Daniels for contributing their work. Erma Gay Jones, for contributing the memories of others—her students, and my heroes. Pearl students, teachers, administrators, and staff, as well as parents and community leaders, who endured and together grew stronger through tragedy. And last but in no way least, Dr. Steve Jackson and Allen Stephens, for their spiritual guidance during and after October 1, 1997.

Source Notes

Chapter One

1. Dan Korem's work relevant to this book are: *Suburban Gangs—The Affluent Rebels* (1994); *The Art of Profiling—Reading People Right the First Time* (1997); *Rage of the Random Actor—Disarming Catastrophic Acts and Restoring Lives* (2005).

Chapter Two

1. *Rage of the Random Actor—Disarming Catastrophic Acts and Restoring Lives*, Dan Korem (International Focus Press: Richardson, Texas, 2005), p. 372.

Chapter Three

1. Ibid, p. 198
2. Ibid, p. 204

Chapter Six

1. *Suburban Gangs—The Affluent Rebels*, Dan Korem (International Focus Press: Richardson, Texas, 1994), p. 35.

Chapter Eight

1. Law enforcement was frustrated that agencies wouldn't allocate funds, so Korem agreed to donate training. But, even this was denied by commanders who didn't recognize the severity of the newsthreat.

Chapter Nine

1. *Rage of the Random Actor—Disarming Catastrophic Acts and Restoring Lives*, p. 221–236. It has been modified from the original for this text.

Chapter Ten

1. Ibid, p. 237–243. It has been modified from the original for this text.

Chapter Eleven
1. "At Last, Facing Down Bullies (and Their Enablers), Perri Klass, M.D., *The New York Times*, June 9, 2009
2. Ibid.
3. Ibid.
4. Ibid.
5. *Suburban Gangs—The Affluent Rebels*, p. 64–65.
6. *Rage of the Random Actor—Disarming Catastrophic Acts and Restoring Lives*, p. 394–399.

Chapter Twelve
1. Ibid, p. 197.
2. Ibid, p. 204–205.
3. Ibid, p. 250–255.

Additional Resources
Related to *If Only I Had Known*

Published and Available from IFP

THE ART OF PROFILING
Reading People Right The First Time
Dan Korem

More people have been trained to use the *Korem Profiling System* than any other on-the-spot profiling system in the world. Hailed by experts around the globe, this landmark text will show you how to profile people within just a few minutes of interaction—*even if you can't speak their language.* Answer four direct questions in your mind about someone and you obtain a 2-page profile that identifies how a person is likely to: communicate • perform tasks • make decisions . . . as well as a person's likely strengths • shortcomings • general tendencies. The profile then tells you how to best interact with that person, sell/present ideas or products, or address a confrontation. Based upon sound science, you will learn how to profile people with systematic accuracy that extends beyond reading body language and avoids stereotyping, like racial profiling. Recommended for any application where you interact with

others, including leading teams; recruiting and hiring; sales and negotiations; education; multi-cultural interactions; security, law enforcement and military environments; recruiting and coaching athletes, even personal relationships and raising children.

"A rare find . . . A masterful text." *From Foreword by James T. Reese, Ph.D,, former member FBI Behavioral Sciences Unit*

"I commanded the Kabul Multi-National Brigade in Afghanistan from July 2003 to Jan. 2004. [I interacted with] 22 different nations that provided troops . . . as well as Afghan authorities, military leadership, elders, religious leaders, nomads and more. The job of a leader is to influence people for mission success and your book assisted me in preparing strategies for the many people I interacted and successfully accomplishing my mission. Thanks." *Colonel Peter Devlin*

256 Pages • Hardbound • Illustrated • $25.95 • ISBN: 0-9639103-3-7

STREETWISE PARENTS, FOOLPROOF KIDS (2d ed.)
Dan Korem

Written for parents, educators, law enforcement, and other professionals who interact with youths (ages 4-17). A section is included on RANDOM ACTOR behavior as it relates to children and parenting. The following issues are also covered in this 2nd edition of this popular book:

- Profile of the youth who is the easiest to deceive and how to help a youth not become that person.
- A simple method for teaching kids how to know if someone is lying or telling the truth.
- How to recognize who is potentially violent and appropriate responses.
- How to distinguish between illusion and reality.
- When it is and isn't appropriate to use deception—i.e., trick play in football versus cheating.
- Guidelines for distinguishing when fantasy and imagination can turn harmful.
- Good versus bad secrets—when it is and isn't appropriate to keep a secret and what to do with harmful secrets.
- Guidelines for healthy decision making and the parents' role.
- Other youth culture issues include: entertainment and news media; drugs/ alcohol; gangs; cults.

    285 Pages • Hardbound • Illustrated • $23.95 • ISBN: 0-9639103-2-9
    Release Date: Early 2010

SUBURBAN GANGS—THE AFFLUENT REBELS
Dan Korem

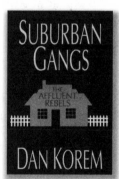

In the mid-1980s, Dan Korem predicted that gangs would appear in affluent communities for the first time in US history. By the late 1980s, his prediction was a fact. By 1994, the typical suburb of 50,000 had 250–500 gang members. Based upon seven years of research in eleven countries, Dan Korem, an internationally recognized gang expert, has produced the first hard-hitting guide to counterattack this unprecedented trend. Laced with riveting accounts and lucidly written for professionals and laymen, *Suburban Gangs* answers the whys while giving real solutions and identifying the following critical information:

- The Missing Protector Strategy: A proven strategy that stops most at-risk behavior, including: gang recruitment, suicide, chronic drug use, teen pregnancy, and truancy. The strategy works effectively in both affluent and inner-city communities. (Korem applied this strategy to over 400 inner-city youths, and not one joined a gang in six years.)
- The profile of the youth most likely to be recruited into an affluent gang.
- Gang types and activities found in affluent communities.
- Disengagement strategy and the eleven reasons why youths disengage from gangs.
- Why skinhead and occultic gangs mysteriously appeared simultaneously in the US and Europe.

- Unique survey of skinhead gang members.
- European parallels that foreshadow gang trends in the US.
- Over 70 photographs show how youth gang cultures in the US and Europe now influence each other for the first time in modern history.

"Recommended strongly for professionals, academics, and the general public."
Library Journal

"It's an excellent read!" *Law Enforcement Training Network*

285 Pages • Hardbound • $24.95 • ISBN: 0-9639103-1-0

PSYCHIC CONFESSION

This classic 1983 documentary, which has been seen by over 100 million people worldwide, contains the only on-camera confession of a cult-like leader who claimed to have powers. It was also Dan Korem's first RANDOM ACTOR case. In 1981, three years after the Jonestown Massacre, James Hydrick, 22, developed a cult-like following in Salt Lake City. He appeared on national television, fooling millions with his claims of psychic powers and alleged healing miracles. Investigative journalist Dan Korem not only exposed on camera how each of Hydrick's tricks worked, such as moving objects without touching them, but his eighteen month investigation also resulted in obtaining a thought-provoking confession of a cult-like figure. After the broadcast, the Department of Health and Human Services purchased the program as it was the first documentary that traced the affects of child abuse through the eyes of an adult.

"It's an altogether fascinating study that transcends the somewhat exploitive subject matter." *Los Angeles Times*

48 minute documentary • DVD format • $24.95

JFK: Breaking the News
Hugh Aynesworth

Hugh Aynesworth, a four-time Pulitzer Prize nominee and bestselling author, assumed he'd be just another spectator as President John F. Kennedy's motorcade rolled through Dealey Plaza on November 22, 1963. But then Lee Harvey Oswald changed the course of history, and Aynesworth's life, as well. He was the only news reporter present at JFK's assassination, as well as Oswald's later capture and his murder by Jack Ruby two days later. That uncanny coincidence helped thrust Aynewworth into the middle of the assassination story, where he has remained, often reluctantly, ever since. He has broken more news about November 22nd and its convoluted aftermath than any other reporter.

JFK: Breaking the News includes many letters and photographs from Aynesworth's archive, including entire pages from his reporter's notebook from the day of the assassination, his interview with Marina Oswald, and more. Related to RANDOM ACTORS, the three key players—Oswald, Ruby, and Garrison—all had the profile.

"Fascinating . . ." *Wall Street Journal*

"Hugh Aynesworth knows more about this tragic story and the reporters who reported it than anyone I know. A splendid piece of work." *Bob Schieffer, Anchor/ Moderator, Face the Nation, CBS News*

"No one — repeat, no one — in America knows more about the Kennedy assassination." *Michael Ruby, former co-editor U.S. News and World Report*

263 Pages • Hardbound • 188 photographs and artifacts • $27.95 • ISBN: 0-9639103-1-0

TO OBTAIN MATERIALS

To obtain any of these materials please see IFP's website (www.ifpinc.com) or write:

INTERNATIONAL FOCUS PRESS
P.O. BOX 1587
RICHARDSON, TEXAS 75083